AF715484

How To Succeed as a Freelancer

Alex Thompson

Published by Side Hustle Success, 2023.

HOW TO SUCCEED AS A FREELANCER

First edition. August 4, 2023.

ISBN: 979-8223427681

Written by Alex Thompson.

Chapter 1: Introduction to the Gig Economy

The world of work is rapidly evolving, and with it comes a significant shift in how people earn a living. Welcome to the gig economy, a dynamic and transformative landscape that has redefined the traditional notions of employment. In this chapter, we will delve into the very core of this exciting and ever-changing realm, exploring what the gig economy truly entails and how freelancers thrive within it.

- Definition of the Gig Economy and Freelance Work

At its essence, the gig economy can be described as a labor market characterized by the prevalence of short-term contracts or freelance work as opposed to permanent employment. In this new paradigm, independent workers, often referred to as gig workers or freelancers, engage in temporary, project-based, or on-demand tasks for various clients or companies. These gigs can range from creative endeavors such as graphic design, writing, and photography to specialized services like web development, consulting, and even ride-sharing.

Freelance work, one of the cornerstones of the gig economy, embodies the spirit of autonomy and flexibility. Freelancers operate as self-employed individuals, offering their skills and expertise to multiple clients or companies, allowing them to create a diverse portfolio of work experiences. This arrangement enables freelancers to have more control over their schedules, choose projects that align with their interests, and explore a variety of industries.

The gig economy's rise can be attributed to a confluence of factors. Rapid advancements in technology have made it easier for individuals to connect with potential clients and employers through digital platforms and online marketplaces. Additionally, many companies are now outsourcing tasks to independent workers to gain access to specialized skills without the overhead costs of hiring full-time employees.

As the gig economy continues to expand, it presents both opportunities and challenges for workers. On the one hand, gig workers can enjoy the freedom to shape their careers, explore diverse opportunities, and achieve a better work-life balance. On the other hand, the lack of traditional benefits and the unpredictability of income can pose risks and uncertainty for those in the gig workforce.

Throughout this book, we will explore how gig economy entrepreneurs can maximize their income potential while minimizing the inherent risks associated with independent work. From financial planning and tax implications to building long-term client relationships and preparing for retirement, we will equip you with the knowledge and strategies you need to thrive as a gig economy entrepreneur.

So, whether you are already a seasoned freelancer or just dipping your toes into the gig economy waters, join us on this journey as we uncover the secrets to becoming a successful gig economy entrepreneur. Let's embark together on the path to maximizing income and minimizing risks in this new world of independent work.

- Overview of the Growing Trend of Independent Workers

The gig economy is not just a passing fad; it represents a significant and enduring shift in the global workforce. As we move further into the 21st century, the trend of independent workers has been steadily gaining momentum. Let's explore some key aspects of this growing phenomenon:

1. Increasing Numbers: Independent workers, including

freelancers, solopreneurs, and temporary workers, make up a substantial portion of the labor force in many countries. According to various studies and reports, the number of gig workers has been steadily rising over the years, and this trend is expected to continue.

2. Diverse Occupations: The gig economy spans across a wide range of occupations and industries. It's not limited to just creative fields like writing or graphic design. Instead, it encompasses professionals in IT, marketing, healthcare, education, and many other sectors. This diversity showcases the flexibility and adaptability of the gig economy model.
3. Millennials and Gen Z: Younger generations, such as millennials and Gen Z, have been at the forefront of embracing gig work. They often value work-life balance, the ability to pursue their passions, and a preference for remote or location-independent work, all of which align with the opportunities provided by the gig economy.
4. Remote Work Revolution: The gig economy has been further accelerated by the remote work revolution. Advancements in communication technology and the COVID-19 pandemic have accelerated the acceptance and adoption of remote work, making gig opportunities more accessible to a global workforce.
5. Entrepreneurial Mindset: The rise of independent workers has also sparked an entrepreneurial mindset among many individuals. Rather than seeking traditional employment, more people are choosing to build their businesses, offering specialized services to clients worldwide.
6. Shift in Company Practices: Even traditional companies have begun to embrace the gig economy model by hiring freelancers for specific projects or tasks. This allows them to tap into a broader talent pool, access specialized skills, and

adjust their workforce according to project demands.

7. Influence on Corporate Culture: The gig economy's influence extends beyond independent workers themselves. It has influenced corporate culture, pushing organizations to adopt more flexible and agile approaches to work, enabling them to adapt to changing market dynamics more effectively.

The growing trend of independent workers signifies a paradigm shift in how people perceive and engage in work. As the gig economy continues to shape the landscape of employment, it opens up new possibilities and opportunities for individuals to chart their own professional paths and create a diverse and fulfilling career journey. However, as the gig economy expands, so do the challenges and complexities that come with it.

- Benefits and Challenges of Working in the Gig Economy

As with any work arrangement, the gig economy offers its fair share of advantages and disadvantages. Let's explore the benefits and challenges that gig economy entrepreneurs may encounter:

Benefits:

1. Flexibility and Autonomy: One of the most significant perks of working in the gig economy is the freedom to choose when, where, and how you work. Gig workers have the flexibility to set their schedules, allowing for a better work-life balance and the ability to pursue personal interests.
2. Diverse Opportunities: The gig economy opens doors to a wide range of opportunities across various industries and niches. Freelancers can explore diverse projects and work with different clients, gaining valuable experiences that can enrich their skill sets and portfolio.

3. Income Control: Gig economy entrepreneurs have the potential to control their income by taking on more projects or higher-paying gigs. With effort and determination, freelancers can increase their earning potential over time.
4. Niche Specialization: Freelancers can focus on their passions and areas of expertise, becoming specialists in their chosen fields. This niche specialization can lead to a more focused client base and potentially higher rates for specialized services.
5. Entrepreneurial Spirit: Working in the gig economy encourages an entrepreneurial mindset. Gig workers have the opportunity to develop their personal brand, market their skills, and build their businesses, all while being in control of their professional destinies.

Challenges:

1. Irregular Income: Unlike traditional employment with a consistent paycheck, gig economy income can be irregular and unpredictable. Fluctuations in demand and payment delays can create financial uncertainty for freelancers.
2. Lack of Benefits: Gig workers often do not receive benefits commonly associated with traditional jobs, such as health insurance, retirement plans, and paid time off. Freelancers must take on the responsibility of securing these benefits independently.
3. Self-Employment Taxes: Freelancers are responsible for paying self-employment taxes, which can be higher than the taxes typically withheld from traditional employees' paychecks. Understanding tax obligations and proper financial planning are crucial for gig economy entrepreneurs.
4. Client Acquisition: Finding and securing clients can be a constant challenge in the gig economy. Freelancers need to

invest time and effort in networking, marketing, and building a strong online presence to attract potential clients.

5. Workload Management: Balancing multiple projects and clients can be overwhelming, leading to potential burnout or subpar work quality. Effective time management and project prioritization are essential to maintain productivity and meet deadlines.
6. Lack of Job Security: Gig workers do not have the stability and job security associated with traditional employment. Freelancers must continually seek new opportunities to sustain their income and career growth.

Navigating the gig economy successfully requires a blend of entrepreneurial spirit, financial acumen, adaptability, and self-discipline.

Chapter 2: Assessing Your Skills and Talents

- Identifying Your Strengths and Areas of Expertise

Knowing your strengths and areas of expertise is a fundamental step in positioning yourself as a successful gig economy entrepreneur. By recognizing what you excel at and what sets you apart from others, you can strategically focus on the opportunities that align with your skills. Here's how you can effectively identify and leverage your strengths:

1. Self-Reflection: Take some time for introspection and self-assessment. Identify the tasks or activities that come naturally to you and bring you joy. Consider your past experiences, both personal and professional, and determine the areas where you have consistently excelled.
2. Seek Feedback: Reach out to colleagues, friends, or mentors for honest feedback about your strengths and skills. Sometimes, others can see qualities in us that we may not recognize ourselves.
3. Analyze Past Successes: Review your previous projects or work experiences where you achieved outstanding results. Identify the skills and qualities that contributed to those successes.
4. Passion and Motivation: Take note of the tasks or subjects that ignite your passion and keep you motivated. Passion can drive excellence, and pursuing work that excites you can lead to more fulfilling gigs.
5. SWOT Analysis: Conduct a SWOT (Strengths, Weaknesses, Opportunities, Threats) analysis of yourself as a gig worker. This analysis will help you understand where your strengths lie and how you can capitalize on them.

6. Niche Specialization: Consider focusing on a specific niche or industry where your strengths align with market demand. Becoming an expert in a particular area can make you more attractive to potential clients seeking specialized services.
7. Adaptability: While identifying your strengths, also acknowledge areas where you are adaptable and willing to learn. The gig economy rewards individuals who can embrace new challenges and acquire new skills as needed.

By gaining a clear understanding of your strengths and areas of expertise, you can effectively market yourself to potential clients and position yourself as a valuable asset in the gig economy. Remember that self-assessment is an ongoing process, and as you gain more experience and feedback, your perception of your strengths may evolve. Stay open to growth and continuous improvement to thrive in the dynamic world of gig work.

- Exploring Market Demand for Your Skills in the Gig Economy

As a gig economy entrepreneur, it's essential to align your skills and talents with the market demand. Understanding the current trends and needs of potential clients can help you make informed decisions about the services you offer and identify profitable opportunities. Here are some steps to explore the market demand for your skills:

1. Research Online Job Marketplaces: Explore popular freelance platforms and job marketplaces to analyze the demand for services similar to yours. Look for the number of job postings and projects related to your expertise. Pay attention to the types of projects that receive more attention and higher rates.
2. Monitor Industry Publications and Websites: Keep yourself

updated with industry-specific publications, websites, and forums. These sources often discuss emerging trends, skill requirements, and the demand for specific services within your niche.

3. Engage in Networking: Attend industry events, webinars, and online networking groups to connect with potential clients and fellow freelancers. Engaging in discussions will give you insights into the challenges faced by clients and the skills they seek in freelancers.
4. Analyze Competitor Activity: Study the work of other freelancers or businesses offering similar services. Observe their pricing, portfolio, and client reviews. This analysis can help you identify gaps in the market and unique selling points for your services.
5. Conduct Surveys or Interviews: If possible, conduct surveys or interviews with your target audience to gather direct feedback about their needs and pain points. This firsthand information can guide you in tailoring your services to meet client expectations.
6. Leverage Social Media: Use social media platforms to engage with your target audience and gain insights into their preferences. Participate in relevant discussions, answer questions, and share valuable content to establish yourself as an authority in your field.
7. Stay Agile and Adaptable: The gig economy is dynamic and constantly evolving. Be prepared to adapt your skill set based on changing market demands and emerging technologies.

By thoroughly exploring the market demand for your skills, you can position yourself strategically to offer services that clients are actively seeking. Utilize the information you gather to refine your offerings, set competitive rates, and develop a compelling pitch to attract potential clients in the competitive gig economy landscape.

- Niche Specialization and Finding Your Competitive Advantage

In the vast and diverse gig economy, standing out from the crowd is crucial to attracting clients and building a successful freelancing career. Niche specialization allows you to focus on a specific area of expertise, making you an expert in your chosen field. Here's how you can find your niche and leverage it to gain a competitive advantage:

1. Evaluate Your Unique Value Proposition: Determine what sets you apart from other freelancers with similar skills. Identify your unique strengths, experiences, and perspectives that can add value to your clients' projects. Your value proposition should resonate with potential clients and address their pain points.
2. Assess Market Demand: Look for areas within your skill set that align with the current market demand. Focus on the industries or niches where your expertise is in high demand, and clients are willing to pay a premium for specialized services.
3. Research Your Target Audience: Understand your target clients and their specific needs. Tailor your services to address their pain points and challenges, positioning yourself as the go-to expert in solving their problems.
4. Be the Go-To Specialist: By specializing in a niche, you position yourself as an authority in that area. Clients seeking specialized services are more likely to trust and hire someone who has a deep understanding of their particular requirements.
5. Build a Strong Portfolio: Showcase your expertise through a

portfolio that highlights your past projects related to your niche. A well-curated portfolio can demonstrate your capabilities and the value you bring to clients.

6. Leverage Testimonials and Reviews: Positive testimonials and client reviews can enhance your credibility and build trust with potential clients. Request feedback from satisfied clients and showcase these endorsements to strengthen your competitive advantage.
7. Continuously Develop Your Skills: Stay up-to-date with industry trends and developments within your niche. Invest in professional development and certifications to ensure you remain at the forefront of your field.
8. Marketing Your Niche: Tailor your marketing efforts to reach your target audience effectively. Utilize social media, content marketing, and targeted advertising to position yourself as the expert in your niche.
9. Provide Excellent Customer Service: Exceptional customer service and client satisfaction can lead to repeat business and referrals. Strive to exceed expectations and cultivate long-term relationships with your clients.

Finding your niche and leveraging it to your advantage is an ongoing process. As you gain experience and expertise, you may fine-tune your niche or expand your services based on evolving market demands. By specializing and honing your competitive advantage, you can position yourself for success in the competitive gig economy landscape.

Chapter 3: Financial Planning for Freelancers

- Creating a Budget for Irregular Income

Managing finances effectively is vital for gig economy entrepreneurs who experience irregular income. Creating a well-thought-out budget is an essential step in gaining control over your finances and ensuring financial stability. Here's how you can create a budget tailored to your unique financial situation:

1. Track Past Income: Start by reviewing your past income streams and earnings as a freelancer. Analyze the variations in income month-to-month or seasonally to identify patterns and understand your income trends.
2. Determine Fixed Expenses: Identify your fixed expenses, such as rent or mortgage, utilities, insurance, and debt repayments. These expenses remain constant regardless of your income fluctuations and should be prioritized in your budget.
3. Account for Variable Expenses: List out discretionary expenses, such as groceries, entertainment, dining out, and non-essential purchases. Allocate a flexible portion of your budget to accommodate these variable expenses.
4. Emergency Fund Allocation: Allocate a portion of your income to build and maintain an emergency fund. This fund should cover three to six months' worth of essential expenses to provide a safety net during lean periods.
5. Consider Irregular Expenses: Anticipate irregular or annual expenses, such as taxes, professional certifications, or equipment upgrades. Set aside funds regularly to prepare for these one-time or periodic expenses.
6. Adopt the 50/30/20 Rule: Consider using the 50/30/20 rule

for budgeting. Allocate 50% of your income to essential expenses, 30% to discretionary spending, and 20% to savings and debt repayment.

7. Prioritize Debt Repayment: If you have outstanding debts, focus on debt repayment to minimize financial burdens. Prioritize high-interest debts first and gradually work towards becoming debt-free.
8. Use Budgeting Tools: Utilize various budgeting apps and tools that can help you track your income and expenses more efficiently. These tools can provide valuable insights into your spending habits and help you stick to your budget.
9. Adjust as Necessary: Be prepared to adjust your budget as your income fluctuates or your financial goals change. Flexibility is essential in a gig economy where income may vary significantly.
10. Review and Reassess Regularly: Regularly review your budget to assess your financial progress and make necessary adjustments. A quarterly or annual review can help you identify areas for improvement and celebrate financial milestones.

Creating a budget tailored to your irregular income as a gig economy entrepreneur can provide peace of mind, reduce financial stress, and pave the way for a more secure financial future. By being proactive and disciplined in managing your finances, you can navigate the ups and downs of freelancing with confidence.

- Emergency Funds and Managing Financial Uncertainty

Financial uncertainty is an inherent part of the gig economy, where income fluctuations are common. To navigate the unpredictability and maintain financial stability, establishing and managing an emergency fund is crucial. Here's how you can build and utilize an emergency fund effectively:

1. The Importance of Emergency Funds: An emergency fund serves as a financial cushion during challenging times. It provides you with a safety net to cover essential expenses in case of unforeseen events, such as a sudden drop in income, unexpected medical expenses, or client payment delays.
2. Set a Target Amount: Determine an ideal amount for your emergency fund based on your fixed expenses. Aim to save three to six months' worth of essential living expenses. Adjust this target based on factors like income stability, industry trends, and personal risk tolerance.
3. Start Small and Be Consistent: If saving a substantial emergency fund seems overwhelming, start with smaller contributions and be consistent in adding to it. Even setting aside a small percentage of each gig's earnings can accumulate over time.
4. Keep the Fund Separate: Maintain your emergency fund in a separate account to prevent accidental spending and make it easily accessible during emergencies. Consider using a high-yield savings account to earn some interest on your savings.
5. Replenish After Withdrawals: If you need to use your emergency fund, make it a priority to replenish it as soon as possible. Continue contributing regularly to bring the fund back to its target level.
6. Assess Risk and Insurance Needs: Evaluate potential risks and consider appropriate insurance coverage to protect yourself and your assets. Health insurance, disability insurance, and liability insurance can offer additional financial security.
7. Diversify Income Streams: Reduce financial uncertainty by diversifying your income streams. Explore opportunities to

work with multiple clients or invest in passive income sources to balance income fluctuations.

8. Create a Contingency Plan: Develop a contingency plan for worst-case scenarios, such as an extended period of low income. Outline actions you can take, such as cutting discretionary spending or exploring temporary part-time work, to tide you over challenging times.
9. Seek Professional Advice: If you're unsure about financial planning or investment strategies, consider consulting a financial advisor or accountant. Their expertise can help you make informed decisions and optimize your emergency fund and overall financial planning.
10. Stay Mindful of Spending: Remain mindful of your spending habits and avoid unnecessary expenses. Being financially conscious can free up resources to contribute to your emergency fund and support your financial well-being.

An emergency fund provides a sense of security and confidence in the face of financial uncertainty. By prioritizing your fund's growth and diligently managing your finances, you can navigate the gig economy with greater resilience and peace of mind.

- Setting Financial Goals and Tracking Progress

As a gig economy entrepreneur, setting clear financial goals is essential to achieve both short-term and long-term financial success. Without traditional employment benefits, it's crucial to proactively plan for your financial future. Here's how you can set financial goals and effectively track your progress:

1. Define Specific Goals: Set clear and measurable financial objectives that align with your overall aspirations. Whether it's paying off debts, saving for retirement, or buying

equipment for your business, articulate your goals in precise terms.

2. Prioritize Goals: Rank your financial goals based on their importance and urgency. Focus on one or two primary objectives at a time to maintain focus and avoid feeling overwhelmed.
3. Establish Realistic Timelines: Set reasonable timelines for achieving your financial goals. Consider factors like your income level, expenses, and potential fluctuations when determining time frames.
4. Break Goals into Milestones: Divide larger goals into smaller milestones. Breaking down your objectives into manageable steps can make them more achievable and provide a sense of progress along the way.
5. Create a Budget to Support Goals: Your budget should be aligned with your financial goals. Allocate funds to each goal category to ensure steady progress in achieving them.
6. Use SMART Goals: Apply the SMART criteria (Specific, Measurable, Achievable, Relevant, Time-bound) to refine your financial objectives. This approach helps ensure your goals are well-defined and within reach.
7. Monitor and Adjust: Regularly review your progress towards each goal. Analyze your budget and financial habits to see if you're on track. If necessary, adjust your strategies to stay in line with your objectives.
8. Celebrate Milestones: Celebrate your achievements as you reach milestones along the way. Rewarding yourself can provide motivation to keep working towards your larger financial goals.
9. Automate Savings and Investments: Simplify the process of saving and investing by setting up automatic transfers. Automating contributions to your emergency fund,

retirement accounts, or investment portfolios ensures consistency.

10. Seek Accountability and Support: Share your financial goals with a trusted friend, family member, or mentor who can hold you accountable. Discussing your progress with someone can offer valuable feedback and encouragement.

Remember that financial goals can evolve over time as your circumstances change. Be adaptable and open to revising your objectives when necessary. Staying committed to your financial plan and tracking your progress will empower you to take charge of your financial future in the gig economy.

Chapter 4: Tax Implications for Independent Workers

• Understanding Self-Employment Taxes

As an independent worker in the gig economy, it's essential to have a clear understanding of self-employment taxes. Unlike traditional employees, freelancers are considered self-employed, which means they are responsible for paying both the employer and employee portions of certain taxes. Here's what you need to know about self-employment taxes:

1. Self-Employment Tax Rate: Self-employment taxes consist of Social Security and Medicare taxes, commonly known as FICA taxes. As of the time of writing, the self-employment tax rate is 15.3% of your net earnings. This rate is subject to change, so be sure to check the latest tax laws.
2. Components of Self-Employment Tax: a. Social Security Tax: This tax component is 12.4% of your net earnings up to a certain income threshold. In 2021, the threshold is $142,800 (subject to change in subsequent years). b. Medicare Tax: The Medicare tax is 2.9% of your net earnings, with no income cap.
3. Net Earnings Calculation: Net earnings for self-employment tax purposes are calculated by deducting allowable business expenses from your total self-employment income.
4. Filing Schedule: As a freelancer, you will need to file an annual tax return and pay self-employment taxes throughout the year. Estimated tax payments are typically required on a quarterly basis if you expect to owe more than a certain amount in taxes.
5. Form 1040 Schedule SE: To report and calculate your self-

employment taxes, you'll use Form 1040 Schedule SE. This form helps you determine the amount of self-employment tax owed.

6. Deductible Business Expenses: The good news is that as a self-employed individual, you can deduct various business-related expenses, which can reduce your taxable income and, consequently, your self-employment tax liability. Common deductible expenses include office supplies, equipment, business travel, and professional services.
7. Keep Accurate Records: To ensure accurate tax reporting and claim all eligible deductions, it's essential to keep detailed and organized records of your business income and expenses.
8. Consider Hiring a Tax Professional: Given the complexity of self-employment taxes, working with a tax professional or an accountant can be highly beneficial. A tax expert can help you navigate tax laws, identify deductions, and ensure compliance with tax regulations.
9. Self-Employment Tax Planning: Plan ahead for your tax obligations by setting aside a portion of your income for taxes and making timely estimated tax payments to avoid potential penalties.

Understanding self-employment taxes is crucial for managing your finances as an independent worker. By staying informed about tax laws and planning for your tax obligations, you can effectively manage your tax liabilities and keep your financial matters in order as a gig economy entrepreneur.

- Deductions and Write-offs for Freelancers

As a freelancer in the gig economy, you have the advantage of being able to deduct various business-related expenses, which can significantly reduce your taxable income and lower your tax liability. Here are some common deductions and write-offs that freelancers can take advantage of:

1. Home Office Expenses: If you have a dedicated space in your home used exclusively for business, you can claim a deduction for home office expenses. This includes a portion of rent or mortgage, utilities, insurance, and maintenance expenses.
2. Business Supplies: The cost of office supplies, such as stationery, printer ink, software subscriptions, and other materials necessary for your freelance work, can be deducted.
3. Equipment and Technology: Expenses for business equipment, such as laptops, cameras, printers, and other tools used for your freelancing work, can be written off as deductions.
4. Business Travel: When you travel for work-related purposes, you can deduct expenses such as transportation (e.g., airfare, mileage), lodging, meals, and other incidentals.
5. Professional Services: Fees paid to lawyers, accountants, and other professional services directly related to your freelancing work can be deducted.
6. Health Insurance Premiums: Self-employed individuals can deduct health insurance premiums for themselves, their spouses, and dependents. This deduction can also include long-term care insurance.
7. Self-Employment Taxes: As mentioned earlier, you can deduct the employer portion of self-employment taxes (Social Security and Medicare taxes) when calculating your taxable income.
8. Continuing Education: Expenses for courses, workshops, or certifications that enhance your skills and knowledge relevant to your freelancing work may be deductible.
9. Subcontractor Payments: If you hire subcontractors to assist

with specific projects, their payments are deductible business expenses.

10. Marketing and Advertising: Costs associated with promoting your freelancing services, such as website hosting, online advertising, business cards, and marketing materials, can be deducted.
11. Business Meals and Entertainment: A portion of business-related meals and entertainment expenses can be deductible, typically up to 50% of the total cost.

It's essential to keep accurate records of your expenses and retain receipts to support your deductions. Consider using accounting software or apps to track your business expenses efficiently. Additionally, consult with a tax professional to ensure you understand which deductions are applicable to your specific freelancing business and to maximize your tax savings while staying compliant with tax laws.

By taking advantage of these deductions and write-offs, you can optimize your tax situation and retain more of your hard-earned income as a gig economy entrepreneur.

- Working with an Accountant or Tax Professional

Navigating the complexities of taxes as a freelancer in the gig economy can be challenging. Engaging the services of an experienced accountant or tax professional can provide significant benefits and peace of mind. Here's how working with a tax professional can support your financial success:

1. Expertise in Self-Employment Taxes: Tax professionals specialize in tax laws and regulations, including those specific to self-employed individuals. They can help you understand

your tax obligations, deductions, and credits, maximizing your tax savings while ensuring compliance.

2. Personalized Tax Planning: An accountant can develop a personalized tax plan tailored to your unique financial situation and business needs. This includes estimating quarterly tax payments to avoid underpayment penalties and strategic planning for deductions.
3. Maximizing Deductions: A tax professional can identify deductions and write-offs that you may not be aware of. They can help you take advantage of every eligible deduction, optimizing your tax benefits.
4. Reducing Risk of Errors: Tax returns for self-employed individuals can be more complex than those for traditional employees. A tax professional can minimize the risk of errors, reducing the likelihood of audits or other tax-related issues.
5. Timely and Accurate Filing: With a tax professional's guidance, you can ensure that your tax returns are filed accurately and submitted on time, avoiding late-filing penalties.
6. Handling IRS Communications: If you receive any correspondence from the IRS or tax authorities, a tax professional can represent you and communicate with them on your behalf, providing guidance and resolving any tax-related matters.
7. Long-Term Financial Planning: Beyond tax season, an accountant can assist with long-term financial planning, such as retirement savings strategies and investment advice.
8. Peace of Mind: Knowing that your taxes are being handled by a qualified professional can provide you with peace of mind, allowing you to focus on your freelancing work without the stress of tax complexities.

When selecting a tax professional, consider the following:

- Look for someone with experience working with freelancers and individuals in the gig economy.
- Check their credentials and certifications, such as Certified Public Accountant (CPA) or Enrolled Agent (EA).
- Seek referrals from other freelancers or colleagues to find a reputable and trustworthy tax professional.

Remember that while a tax professional can offer valuable guidance, you remain ultimately responsible for your tax returns. Stay involved in the process, ask questions, and keep them informed about changes in your financial situation throughout the year.

By partnering with a qualified accountant or tax professional, you can optimize your financial planning, minimize tax liabilities, and secure a strong financial foundation as a successful gig economy entrepreneur.

Chapter 5: Managing Business Expenses

- Differentiating Personal and Business Expenses

As a gig economy entrepreneur, it's crucial to distinguish between personal and business expenses to maintain accurate financial records, maximize tax deductions, and ensure compliance with tax regulations. Here's how you can effectively differentiate between the two:

1. Set Up Separate Bank Accounts: Establishing separate bank accounts for personal and business use is a fundamental step in managing expenses. Use the business account exclusively for business-related transactions to keep finances distinct and organized.
2. Maintain Detailed Records: Keep meticulous records of all expenses incurred for your freelancing work. Save receipts, invoices, and any other relevant documentation to substantiate business expenses for tax purposes.
3. Create a Budget: Develop a clear and comprehensive budget that outlines business-related expenses separately from personal spending. A well-structured budget will help you track cash flow and stay on top of your financial situation.
4. Understand Business Expenses: Familiarize yourself with the types of expenses that are considered deductible business expenses, such as office supplies, equipment, marketing, travel, and professional services. Be aware of the applicable tax regulations and limitations for each category.
5. Avoid Personal Expenses in Business Accounts: Be vigilant about not using your business account for personal expenses. Mixing personal and business transactions can make it challenging to identify and manage your actual business expenses accurately.

6. Reimburse Yourself for Business Expenses: If you inadvertently use personal funds for a business expense, reimburse yourself from the business account. This will help maintain clear records and prevent confusion.
7. Use Accounting Software: Implement accounting software or apps to track income and expenses automatically. These tools can help you categorize transactions correctly and generate reports for tax preparation.
8. Consult with a Tax Professional: If you are unsure about classifying certain expenses, seek advice from a tax professional. An accountant can guide you on proper expense categorization and help you identify eligible tax deductions.
9. Review Regularly: Periodically review your financial records to ensure accuracy and identify any misclassified expenses. This practice will help you catch errors early and make corrections promptly.
10. Educate Yourself: Stay informed about tax laws and regulations related to business expenses. The more you understand the rules, the better you can manage your finances and optimize your tax benefits.

By keeping personal and business expenses separate and maintaining diligent records, you'll be better positioned to manage your business finances efficiently. Accurate expense management enables you to take advantage of eligible deductions, reduce tax liabilities, and make informed financial decisions that support the growth and success of your gig economy business.

- Strategies for Cost-Cutting and Efficient Spending

As a gig economy entrepreneur, adopting cost-cutting strategies and implementing efficient spending practices can help you maximize your profits and build a financially sustainable freelancing career. Here are some effective strategies to manage your business expenses efficiently:

1. Budget Wisely: Create a detailed budget that outlines all your anticipated business expenses and revenue. Regularly review and update the budget to identify areas where you can reduce costs and allocate resources more effectively.
2. Prioritize Essential Expenses: Distinguish between essential and non-essential expenses. Prioritize spending on items crucial for your business's success while cutting back on non-essential expenditures.
3. Negotiate with Suppliers: Negotiate with suppliers, vendors, and service providers to secure better deals and discounts. Building strong relationships with suppliers can lead to more favorable terms and cost savings.
4. Leverage Technology: Use technology to streamline processes and reduce manual work. Utilize productivity tools, project management software, and communication platforms to enhance efficiency and save time.
5. Consider Outsourcing: For tasks that are outside your core expertise, consider outsourcing to freelancers or agencies. Outsourcing can be cost-effective and allow you to focus on high-value activities.
6. Track Expense Receipts: Keep track of all business-related expense receipts to ensure accurate record-keeping and to maximize tax deductions.
7. Reevaluate Subscriptions: Regularly review your subscriptions and memberships. Cancel those that are underutilized or no longer relevant to your business.
8. Optimize Marketing Spending: Analyze the effectiveness of your marketing efforts and invest in strategies that deliver the highest return on investment (ROI). Focus on digital

marketing channels that target your ideal clients.

9. Utilize Free and Low-Cost Tools: Take advantage of free or affordable software tools and resources that can perform essential business functions. From project management to graphic design, there are numerous cost-effective options available.
10. Bulk Purchase and Discounts: When buying office supplies or equipment, consider purchasing in bulk or taking advantage of discounts offered by vendors.
11. Bartering and Collaborations: Explore opportunities for bartering or collaborations with other freelancers or businesses. Trading services or collaborating on projects can benefit both parties without additional costs.
12. Monitor Cash Flow: Maintain a close eye on your cash flow to identify any potential financial challenges and take proactive measures to address them.
13. Regularly Review Expenses: Regularly review your business expenses to identify trends and areas where you can cut costs or optimize spending.

By implementing these strategies, you can ensure that your business operates efficiently while minimizing unnecessary expenses. Efficient spending and cost-cutting will contribute to a healthier bottom line, increased profitability, and improved financial stability as you thrive in the gig economy.

- Leveraging Technology and Tools for Financial Management

In the digital age, gig economy entrepreneurs have access to a wide range of technology and tools that can significantly enhance financial management. Embracing these digital solutions can streamline processes, improve efficiency, and provide valuable insights into your financial health. Here are some ways to leverage technology for effective financial management:

1. Accounting Software: Use accounting software to track income, expenses, and invoices. These tools automate financial tasks, generate reports, and provide a clear overview of your financial position.
2. Expense Tracking Apps: Utilize expense tracking apps on your mobile device to capture receipts, categorize expenses, and maintain organized records on the go.
3. Digital Payment Solutions: Embrace digital payment platforms to receive payments from clients quickly and securely. These platforms often offer various payment options, making it easier for clients to pay you.
4. Budgeting Apps: Employ budgeting apps to create and monitor your budget effectively. These apps can send alerts for overspending and help you stay on track with financial goals.
5. Cloud Storage: Store financial documents and records in cloud storage platforms. This ensures data security, easy access, and the ability to share documents with relevant parties when necessary.
6. Financial Dashboards: Use financial dashboard tools to visualize key financial metrics, such as income, expenses, and profit trends. These dashboards offer real-time insights to aid in decision-making.
7. Online Invoicing: Generate and send professional invoices using online invoicing tools. These platforms often integrate with payment gateways, simplifying the invoicing and payment process.
8. Time Tracking Software: For freelancers who bill hourly or on a project basis, time tracking software can accurately

record billable hours and assist with client invoicing.

9. Tax Preparation Software: Utilize tax preparation software to simplify tax filing processes and ensure accurate reporting of income and deductions.
10. Personal Finance Apps: Employ personal finance apps to manage personal finances separately from your business finances. This clear separation can prevent confusion and improve overall financial management.
11. Financial Analytics: Use financial analytics tools to analyze your financial data and identify trends, patterns, and areas for improvement in your business finances.
12. Virtual Meetings and Collaboration Tools: Reduce travel costs by leveraging virtual meeting platforms and collaboration tools for client meetings and team communication.
13. Automatic Savings Apps: Consider using automatic savings apps that round up purchases and save the difference. These small savings can accumulate over time and contribute to your emergency fund or investments.

By integrating technology and tools into your financial management practices, you can enhance productivity, accuracy, and organization in your freelancing business. Take advantage of the vast array of digital solutions available to optimize your financial processes and position yourself for success in the dynamic world of the gig economy.

Chapter 6: Building a Strong Online Presence

- Creating a Professional Website and Portfolio

In the gig economy, a strong online presence is crucial for attracting clients, showcasing your expertise, and building credibility. Creating a professional website and portfolio is an essential step to establish yourself as a reputable freelancer. Here's how to craft a compelling online presence:

1. Choose a Professional Domain Name: Select a domain name that reflects your name or business identity. Keep it simple, memorable, and relevant to your freelancing services.
2. Invest in Quality Web Hosting: Opt for reliable web hosting to ensure your website is accessible and fast-loading. A professional web hosting service enhances user experience and boosts search engine rankings.
3. Design a Clean and User-Friendly Website: Create a visually appealing website with a clean and intuitive design. Make it easy for visitors to navigate, find information about your services, and contact you.
4. Showcase Your Work: Your portfolio is a showcase of your best work and accomplishments. Include high-quality samples, case studies, or testimonials that demonstrate your expertise and the value you offer to clients.
5. Craft a Compelling About Me Page: Use the About Me page to share your story, background, and passion for your freelancing work. This page helps clients connect with you on a personal level.
6. Highlight Services and Specializations: Clearly outline the services you offer and any niche specializations you have. This

clarity helps potential clients understand how you can meet their needs.

7. Optimize for Search Engines: Implement basic search engine optimization (SEO) practices to improve your website's visibility in search engine results. Use relevant keywords, meta tags, and create valuable content.
8. Mobile-Friendly Design: Ensure that your website is responsive and adapts to different screen sizes. A mobile-friendly design is essential as many clients access websites from their smartphones and tablets.
9. Include Contact Information: Make it easy for clients to get in touch with you. Provide multiple contact options, such as an email address, phone number, and a contact form.
10. Regularly Update Content: Keep your website fresh and engaging by regularly updating your content. Share blog posts, industry insights, or project updates to demonstrate your expertise and maintain visitor interest.
11. Display Social Proof: Incorporate social proof elements like client testimonials, reviews, and endorsements from reputable sources. Positive feedback builds trust with potential clients.
12. Integrate Social Media: Include links to your social media profiles on your website. Engage with your audience on social platforms and share valuable content related to your freelancing niche.
13. Implement Security Measures: Protect your website and visitors' data by implementing security measures, such as SSL certificates and regular backups.

Your website and portfolio serve as a virtual business card, representing your professionalism and expertise to potential clients. Building a strong online presence can significantly impact your success as a gig economy entrepreneur, helping you attract more clients and establish lasting relationships in the industry.

- Utilizing Social Media for Networking and Marketing

Social media has become an invaluable tool for freelancers to network with potential clients, showcase their skills, and market their services. Leveraging social media platforms effectively can expand your reach, enhance your online presence, and boost your freelancing career. Here's how to utilize social media for networking and marketing:

1. Choose the Right Platforms: Identify the social media platforms most relevant to your freelancing niche and target audience. Focus on platforms where your potential clients are active, such as LinkedIn, Twitter, Instagram, or Facebook.
2. Create a Consistent Brand Identity: Maintain a consistent brand identity across all your social media profiles. Use the same profile picture, bio, and handle to create a cohesive and recognizable online presence.
3. Engage with Your Audience: Actively engage with your followers by responding to comments, messages, and mentions. Show genuine interest in your audience, answer questions, and participate in discussions related to your field.
4. Share Valuable Content: Share content that showcases your expertise and provides value to your audience. This could include informative blog posts, industry insights, helpful tips, and updates on your latest projects.
5. Utilize Visual Content: Visual content, such as infographics, videos, and eye-catching images, tends to attract more attention on social media. Use visuals to complement your written content and make it more shareable.
6. Participate in Relevant Groups and Chats: Join industry-specific groups or Twitter chats related to your freelancing

niche. Engage in conversations, share insights, and establish yourself as a knowledgeable professional.

7. Collaborate and Network: Collaborate with other freelancers or professionals in complementary fields. Partnering with others can extend your network and open up new opportunities.
8. Use Hashtags Strategically: Research and use relevant hashtags to increase the discoverability of your posts. Hashtags help your content reach a wider audience beyond your immediate followers.
9. Showcase Your Portfolio: Share your portfolio or links to your best work on social media to demonstrate your capabilities. Visual samples can capture the attention of potential clients.
10. Monitor Analytics: Utilize social media analytics tools to track engagement, reach, and audience demographics. Analyzing data will help you understand what content resonates best with your audience and optimize your social media strategy.
11. Stay Consistent and Regular: Regularly update your social media profiles with fresh content. Consistency is key to maintaining an active and engaged audience.
12. Be Authentic and Personable: Showcase your personality and authenticity in your social media interactions. People connect with real individuals, so be approachable and personable in your online presence.
13. Promote Your Website and Blog: Drive traffic to your professional website and blog by sharing links to your valuable content on social media. This will increase your website's visibility and authority.

By leveraging social media effectively, you can build valuable connections, establish yourself as an industry expert, and attract potential clients to your freelance services. Remember that social media is not just a promotional tool but also an opportunity to engage, network, and add value to your online community.

- Online Platforms and Marketplaces for Freelancers

In the gig economy, online platforms and marketplaces provide freelancers with access to a vast pool of potential clients and job opportunities. These platforms facilitate connections between freelancers and clients, making it easier to showcase skills, find projects, and establish a reputation in the industry. Here are some popular online platforms and marketplaces for freelancers:

1. Upwork: Upwork is one of the largest freelance marketplaces, offering a wide range of projects across various industries. Freelancers can create profiles, bid on projects, and build ongoing relationships with clients.
2. Fiverr: Fiverr is a platform where freelancers offer services in the form of "gigs" at various price points. It is well-suited for creatives, writers, designers, and other professionals with specialized skills.
3. Freelancer: Freelancer.com is a global platform where freelancers can bid on projects posted by clients worldwide. It covers a wide range of skills and industries.
4. Guru: Guru is a platform that connects freelancers with businesses seeking their services. Freelancers can showcase their portfolios, pitch proposals, and collaborate with clients.
5. Toptal: Toptal is a curated network of elite freelance talent, specializing in software development, design, finance, and project management. It has a rigorous screening process for freelancers.

6. 99designs: 99designs is a platform specifically for graphic designers. Clients can run design contests, and freelancers can participate and showcase their creative skills.
7. PeoplePerHour: PeoplePerHour allows freelancers to create profiles, define their hourly rates, and offer services in various categories. It's popular for both one-time projects and ongoing work.
8. SimplyHired: SimplyHired aggregates freelance job listings from various websites, making it a convenient platform to explore diverse opportunities.
9. FlexJobs: FlexJobs is a job board that curates remote and flexible job opportunities, including freelance positions across different industries.
10. LinkedIn ProFinder: LinkedIn ProFinder is a marketplace within LinkedIn that connects businesses with freelance professionals. Freelancers can showcase their expertise and respond to project requests.
11. Behance: Behance is a platform for creative professionals to showcase their portfolios, gain exposure, and connect with potential clients and collaborators.
12. Remote.co: Remote.co is a platform focused on remote work opportunities, including freelance and contract positions across different fields.

When using online platforms and marketplaces, freelancers should consider the following:

- Research the platform's fees and payment terms to ensure they align with your financial goals.
- Create a compelling profile that highlights your skills, experience, and achievements.
- Customize proposals and bids to demonstrate your understanding of the client's needs.

- Prioritize platforms with strong user reviews and reputable clients to ensure a positive experience.

Diversifying your presence across multiple platforms can increase your visibility and access to a broader range of clients and projects. However, it's essential to maintain professionalism and deliver high-quality work to build a successful freelancing career on these platforms.

Chapter 7: Networking and Finding Clients

- Importance of Networking in the Gig Economy

Networking plays a pivotal role in the success of gig economy entrepreneurs. In a digital landscape where opportunities are abundant but competition is fierce, building and maintaining a strong professional network is essential for finding clients, securing projects, and fostering career growth. Here's why networking holds tremendous significance in the gig economy:

1. Access to Opportunities: Networking opens doors to new opportunities that may not be publicly advertised. Through connections, freelancers gain access to exclusive job leads, referrals, and projects that match their skills and expertise.
2. Building Trust and Credibility: Meeting and engaging with clients and fellow freelancers face-to-face or online helps build trust and credibility. Personal interactions demonstrate professionalism, reliability, and a commitment to one's craft.
3. Word-of-Mouth Referrals: Satisfied clients and professional contacts are likely to refer freelancers to others in need of similar services. Positive word-of-mouth referrals can lead to a steady stream of clients without extensive marketing efforts.
4. Learning from Peers: Networking allows freelancers to connect with peers in the same industry or field. By sharing experiences, best practices, and insights, freelancers can learn from each other and improve their skills and knowledge.
5. Collaborative Opportunities: Networking often leads to collaborative ventures with other freelancers or businesses. Collaborations can expand the scope of services offered and open doors to new markets and clientele.

6. Industry Insights and Trends: Engaging with fellow professionals and industry leaders exposes freelancers to the latest trends, innovations, and market demands. Staying informed helps freelancers adapt and stay relevant in a rapidly changing gig economy landscape.
7. Overcoming Isolation: Freelancing can sometimes be isolating, especially for those who work remotely. Networking provides freelancers with a sense of community, reducing feelings of isolation and fostering a supportive environment.
8. Receiving Feedback: Networking facilitates interactions with clients and fellow freelancers, which can lead to valuable feedback. Constructive criticism and positive feedback aid in improving the quality of services and customer satisfaction.
9. Personal Branding: Active networking allows freelancers to build and maintain their personal brand. By showcasing expertise and sharing valuable insights, freelancers can position themselves as authorities in their respective fields.
10. Long-Term Relationships: Networking isn't just about immediate gains; it nurtures long-term relationships. Clients and contacts cultivated through networking may return for repeat projects or refer others to the freelancer in the future.
11. Tapping into Hidden Job Market: Many job opportunities in the gig economy are not publicly advertised. Networking provides a way to tap into this hidden job market, increasing the chances of finding high-quality and exclusive opportunities.
12. Emotional Support and Motivation: Networking communities can offer emotional support, advice, and motivation during challenging times. Connecting with others who face similar career challenges can provide a sense of camaraderie and encouragement.

In the gig economy, where personal connections and reputation can make a significant difference, networking is an invaluable tool for freelancers. Engaging in networking activities, both online and offline, can lead to a flourishing career, increased client base, and a strong professional identity in the ever-evolving world of independent work.

- Building Relationships with Potential Clients and Partners

Building strong relationships with potential clients and partners is a key aspect of networking in the gig economy. Creating meaningful connections goes beyond transactional interactions; it involves nurturing trust, understanding clients' needs, and showcasing the value you bring to the table. Here's how to build relationships with potential clients and partners effectively:

1. Understand Client Needs: Listen actively and ask probing questions to understand your potential clients' goals, pain points, and challenges. Tailor your services or offerings to address their specific needs and provide relevant solutions.
2. Offer Value First: Show your expertise and provide value upfront. Share insights, resources, or tips related to your field of expertise. Demonstrating your knowledge and willingness to help without expectation can foster trust and credibility.
3. Personalize Your Approach: Avoid a one-size-fits-all approach when engaging with potential clients or partners. Tailor your interactions to match their communication style and preferences.
4. Be Reliable and Responsive: Timely and reliable communication is essential to building trust. Respond promptly to inquiries, deliver on promises, and be transparent about project timelines and deliverables.
5. Follow Up and Follow Through: After initial interactions, follow up with potential clients and partners to maintain

engagement. Follow through on commitments and maintain a professional and courteous demeanor throughout the process.

6. Seek Long-Term Partnerships: Instead of focusing solely on one-off transactions, aim to establish long-term partnerships. Building lasting relationships can lead to repeat business and referrals.
7. Attend Networking Events: Participate in industry events, conferences, and webinars to connect with potential clients and partners. Engage in conversations and exchange contact information to continue the discussion beyond the event.
8. Utilize Social Media: Social media platforms offer an opportunity to engage with potential clients and partners in a more informal setting. Share valuable content, comment on their posts, and engage in discussions to build rapport.
9. Offer Testimonials and Referrals: If you've worked with satisfied clients or partners, offer to provide testimonials or referrals. Positive reviews can strengthen your reputation and attract new clients.
10. Be Genuine and Authentic: Authenticity is essential in building relationships. Be yourself and show genuine interest in the people you interact with. People are more likely to connect with someone they perceive as authentic.
11. Collaborate on Projects: Consider collaborative projects with potential partners to demonstrate your ability to work well together. Collaborations can lead to mutual benefits and strengthen professional ties.
12. Show Gratitude: Express gratitude for opportunities, referrals, or positive interactions. A simple thank-you can leave a lasting positive impression.
13. Stay Connected: Continue nurturing relationships even after projects or collaborations end. Stay in touch through

occasional check-ins or updates, reinforcing your commitment to the relationship.

Building relationships with potential clients and partners is an ongoing process that requires patience, empathy, and genuine interest in others. By focusing on building meaningful connections, freelancers can create a network of valuable clients and partners who contribute to their success in the gig economy.

- Strategies for Finding New Freelance Opportunities

Finding new freelance opportunities is vital for the growth and sustainability of your gig economy career. Adopting proactive strategies to uncover potential projects and clients can lead to a consistent flow of work and increased success. Here are effective strategies for finding new freelance opportunities:

1. Tap into Your Network: Start by reaching out to your existing network of friends, colleagues, and acquaintances. Let them know about your freelancing services and ask for referrals. Your network can be a valuable source of new opportunities.
2. Online Freelance Platforms: Utilize online freelance platforms such as Upwork, Fiverr, and Freelancer to browse job listings, submit proposals, and connect with clients seeking freelancers in your field.
3. Attend Networking Events: Attend industry-specific networking events, meetups, conferences, and webinars. These gatherings provide valuable opportunities to connect with potential clients, collaborators, and industry peers.
4. Utilize Social Media: Leverage social media platforms to showcase your work, share industry insights, and connect with potential clients. Engage in relevant conversations and

utilize hashtags to increase your visibility.

5. Cold Outreach: Identify potential clients or companies that align with your expertise and send personalized cold emails or direct messages. Clearly communicate the value you can bring to their projects.
6. Collaborate with Other Freelancers: Collaborate with freelancers in complementary fields to expand your service offerings and reach a broader audience. Partnering with others can lead to joint projects and mutual referrals.
7. Optimize Your Website and Portfolio: Ensure your professional website and portfolio are up-to-date, visually appealing, and showcase your best work. This online presence acts as a powerful marketing tool to attract potential clients.
8. Join Freelancer Groups: Participate in online forums, Facebook groups, or LinkedIn communities dedicated to freelancing. Engage in discussions, share your expertise, and connect with potential clients or fellow freelancers.
9. Offer Free or Low-Cost Services: Consider offering a limited number of free or discounted services to build your portfolio and gain testimonials from satisfied clients. This initial investment can lead to more paid opportunities in the future.
10. Monitor Job Boards: Keep an eye on job boards, both industry-specific and general, for freelance opportunities. Websites like ProBlogger, We Work Remotely, and Remote.co often list freelance positions.
11. Reach Out to Past Clients: Reconnect with previous clients and remind them of your availability for new projects. Past clients who were pleased with your work are more likely to hire you again or refer you to others.
12. Offer Workshops or Webinars: Host workshops, webinars, or online courses related to your expertise. These events can attract potential clients who are interested in your skills and

knowledge.

13. Stay Updated on Industry Trends: Continuously educate yourself about industry trends, emerging technologies, and new opportunities. Being up-to-date on the latest developments positions you as a forward-thinking freelancer.

Consistency and persistence are essential when implementing these strategies. Finding new freelance opportunities may take time, but by continuously refining your approach and building relationships, you can open doors to a steady stream of exciting projects and clients in the dynamic world of the gig economy.

Chapter 8: Pricing Your Services

- Determining Your Freelance Rates

Setting the right freelance rates is crucial for striking a balance between attracting clients and valuing your skills and expertise appropriately. Charging competitive yet reasonable rates ensures you receive fair compensation for your work while staying competitive in the gig economy. Here are steps to help you determine your freelance rates:

1. Assess Your Skills and Experience: Take stock of your skills, experience, and qualifications. Consider your level of expertise, the demand for your services, and any specialized knowledge you possess.
2. Research Industry Standards: Research industry standards and the rates charged by other freelancers in your field. Websites, forums, and freelance platforms can be valuable sources of rate information.
3. Calculate Your Costs: Determine your monthly living expenses, business overhead costs, and any taxes you need to cover. Understanding your financial requirements is essential for setting sustainable rates.
4. Define Your Value Proposition: Clarify the unique value you offer to clients. A compelling value proposition justifies higher rates by highlighting the benefits clients will receive from working with you.
5. Consider the Complexity of Projects: Complex and time-consuming projects typically warrant higher rates. Factor in the level of effort, research, and expertise required for each type of project.
6. Evaluate Market Demand: Assess the demand for your services in the current market. If demand is high, you may be

able to set higher rates, but be mindful of staying competitive.

7. Determine Your Desired Income: Set income goals based on your financial aspirations. Calculate how much you want to earn annually and break it down into monthly, weekly, or hourly rates.
8. Assess Your Target Clients: Consider the budget and expectations of your target clients. Higher-end clients may be willing to pay premium rates for exceptional service and results.
9. Test Different Rates: If you're unsure about your rates, consider starting with a mid-range rate and adjusting as you gain experience and feedback from clients.
10. Offer Different Service Packages: Create tiered pricing packages that cater to different client needs and budgets. This approach gives clients options while allowing you to charge higher rates for comprehensive packages.
11. Be Transparent: Clearly communicate your rates to clients from the beginning of your interactions. Transparent pricing helps manage client expectations and reduces the likelihood of misunderstandings later on.
12. Reevaluate Regularly: Periodically review your rates and adjust them as your skills, experience, and market conditions change. Regularly updating your rates ensures you continue to receive fair compensation.
13. Negotiate Thoughtfully: Be open to negotiation but stand firm on the value you provide. Be prepared to justify your rates based on your expertise and the quality of your work.

Remember that setting rates is a balancing act between pricing competitively and valuing your skills appropriately. Avoid underpricing yourself, as this can lead to burnout and undervalue the work you do. Confidence in your abilities and a clear understanding of your worth will guide you in determining rates that are fair, competitive, and reflective of the value you bring to your clients.

- Negotiation Tactics and Handling Pricing Objections

Negotiation is a crucial skill for freelancers to secure fair compensation for their services and maintain healthy client relationships. Handling pricing objections with finesse can lead to successful outcomes and create win-win situations. Here are effective negotiation tactics and strategies for addressing pricing objections:

1. Focus on Value: Emphasize the value your services bring to the client. Clearly articulate how your expertise and skills address their specific needs and deliver exceptional results.
2. Listen Actively: When clients raise pricing objections, listen carefully to their concerns. Understand their budget constraints and expectations to find common ground.
3. Offer Options: Provide flexible pricing options to accommodate different budgets. Present tiered packages with varying levels of service to give clients choices.
4. Highlight Past Successes: Share case studies, testimonials, or examples of previous work that demonstrate the positive outcomes you've achieved for other clients. Social proof can alleviate doubts and objections.
5. Explain the Benefits: Clearly explain the benefits of your services and how they outweigh the investment. Focus on the long-term value your work brings to the client's business or project.
6. Know Your Bottom Line: Be clear about the minimum rate you're willing to accept without compromising the quality of your work. Knowing your bottom line helps you negotiate with confidence.
7. Stay Professional and Positive: Keep the negotiation process

positive and professional. Avoid becoming defensive, and instead, focus on finding a mutually beneficial solution.

8. Offer Add-Ons or Bonuses: Sweeten the deal by including additional services or bonuses at the initial price. This can make your proposal more enticing to clients.
9. Propose a Trial Period: If a client is hesitant about committing to a long-term contract, suggest a trial period to demonstrate the value of your services before committing to a larger project.
10. Find Trade-Offs: If a client insists on a lower rate, consider offering alternative benefits, such as a shorter turnaround time or additional deliverables.
11. Educate Clients: Help clients understand the complexities and effort required to deliver high-quality work. Educating them on the value of your expertise can lead to a greater appreciation for your rates.
12. Stay Confident: Confidence in your abilities and the value you provide is essential during negotiations. Maintain a positive attitude and assert your worth without appearing desperate.
13. Part on Good Terms: If you can't reach an agreement on pricing, part ways amicably and professionally. Keep the door open for future opportunities, as circumstances may change.

Remember that negotiation is not about winning or losing; it's about finding a mutually satisfactory arrangement. By demonstrating the value of your services, offering options, and handling objections with poise, you can navigate negotiations effectively and build lasting relationships with clients in the gig economy.

- Balancing Competitive Pricing with Fair Compensation

Balancing competitive pricing with fair compensation is a delicate challenge for freelancers. While offering competitive rates can attract clients and create opportunities, it's equally important to ensure you are compensated fairly for your expertise and effort. Here are strategies to strike the right balance between competitive pricing and fair compensation:

1. Research Market Rates: Understand the average rates for freelancers in your field and geographic area. Research online platforms, industry associations, and networking groups to gather rate information.
2. Consider Your Experience: Factor in your level of experience, skill set, and expertise when determining your rates. As your experience grows, your rates should reflect the value you bring to the table.
3. Calculate Your Costs: Determine your business expenses, taxes, and living costs to set a minimum rate that covers your financial needs while remaining competitive.
4. Offer Value-Added Services: Differentiate your offerings by including value-added services or bonuses in your packages. These extras can justify higher rates and make your proposals more attractive.
5. Create Tiered Packages: Offer tiered pricing options that cater to different client budgets and requirements. This allows clients to choose a level of service that fits their needs while accommodating your desired compensation.
6. Charge for Customization: If clients request extensive customizations or additional work beyond the initial agreement, consider charging extra for these modifications.
7. Define Scope Clearly: Set clear expectations and define the scope of work in your contracts to prevent scope creep and ensure you are compensated for any additional work

requested by the client.

8. Establish Retainer Agreements: Consider retainer agreements with clients who need ongoing services. Retainers offer stability and recurring income while encouraging long-term relationships.
9. Be Mindful of Discounting: Avoid excessive discounting, as it can undervalue your services and set a precedent for future negotiations. Instead, focus on demonstrating the value you provide.
10. Know Your Worth: Recognize your worth as a professional with specialized skills. Avoid undervaluing yourself to win a project, as this can lead to burnout and dissatisfaction.
11. Communicate Clearly: Be transparent with clients about your rates and the value you offer. Open communication builds trust and ensures both parties are on the same page.
12. Negotiate Thoughtfully: When negotiating, find a balance between meeting client needs and valuing your expertise. Be open to compromise but avoid significantly undercutting your rates.
13. Evaluate Return on Investment: Assess the return on investment for each project. If a lower-paying project offers exposure or valuable connections, it may be worthwhile, but weigh the benefits against the time invested.

Striking the right balance between competitive pricing and fair compensation is a continuous process that evolves as your freelance career progresses. Regularly review your rates, refine your negotiation skills, and maintain a strong understanding of your value in the marketplace. By doing so, you can build a sustainable and fulfilling freelancing career in the gig economy.

Chapter 9: Time Management and Productivity

- Developing Effective Time Management Techniques

In the fast-paced world of freelancing, effective time management is essential for maximizing productivity, meeting deadlines, and maintaining work-life balance. Here are techniques to help you manage your time efficiently as a gig economy entrepreneur:

1. Set Clear Goals: Define your short-term and long-term goals. Break them down into smaller, actionable tasks to create a clear roadmap for your work.
2. Prioritize Tasks: Prioritize your tasks based on their urgency and importance. Focus on high-priority items first to ensure critical deadlines are met.
3. Create a Schedule: Develop a daily or weekly schedule that outlines when you'll work on specific tasks. Stick to your schedule to build consistency and discipline.
4. Use Time Management Tools: Utilize tools like to-do lists, time-tracking apps, and project management software to organize your tasks and monitor your progress.
5. Set Time Limits: Allocate specific time slots for each task to prevent overcommitting and ensure you stay on track throughout the day.
6. Break Tasks into Blocks: Adopt the Pomodoro Technique or similar methods to work in focused blocks of time with short breaks in between. This helps maintain concentration and prevents burnout.
7. Eliminate Distractions: Identify common distractions and take measures to minimize them. Consider using website blockers or turning off notifications during work hours.

8. Delegate When Possible: Delegate non-essential tasks or outsource certain aspects of your work to free up time for high-priority activities.
9. Batch Similar Tasks: Group similar tasks together and tackle them in one go. This method streamlines your workflow and reduces mental switching costs.
10. Learn to Say No: Don't overcommit yourself to projects or tasks that don't align with your goals or values. Learn to say no to opportunities that could stretch you too thin.
11. Avoid Multitasking: Focus on one task at a time to maintain productivity and produce higher-quality work.
12. Take Breaks: Incorporate regular breaks into your schedule to rest and recharge. Stepping away from work can enhance creativity and prevent burnout.
13. Review and Adjust: Regularly review your time management techniques to identify areas for improvement. Be open to adjusting your strategies as your workload or priorities change.

By implementing effective time management techniques, you can make the most of your work hours, boost productivity, and achieve a healthy work-life balance as a gig economy entrepreneur. Consistency and discipline are key to developing habits that lead to increased efficiency and success in your freelance endeavors.

- Tools for Productivity and Project Tracking

As a gig economy entrepreneur, utilizing productivity and project tracking tools can significantly enhance your efficiency and organization. These tools help you manage tasks, stay on top of deadlines, and collaborate with clients and team members. Here are some valuable tools to consider:

1. Task Management Tools:

- Todoist: A powerful task manager with features like due dates, labels, and project organization.
- Trello: A visual project management tool using boards, lists, and cards for easy task tracking.
- Asana: A comprehensive project management platform for organizing and assigning tasks.

1. Time Tracking Apps:

- Toggl: A simple and intuitive time tracking tool to monitor how much time you spend on tasks and projects.
- Harvest: Allows you to track time, manage expenses, and generate invoices for clients.

1. Project Collaboration Platforms:

- Slack: A popular messaging app for real-time communication and collaboration with clients and team members.
- Microsoft Teams: Provides chat, video conferencing, file sharing, and integration with other Microsoft tools.

1. Cloud Storage and File Sharing:

- Google Drive: Offers file storage, sharing, and collaboration with easy access from any device.
- Dropbox: A secure cloud storage solution for sharing large files and collaborating on projects.

1. Note-taking and Organization:

- Evernote: A note-taking app for capturing ideas, organizing

information, and sharing notes with others.
- Notion: Combines note-taking, task management, and databases in one flexible workspace.

1. Password Managers:

- LastPass: A secure password manager to store and generate strong passwords for various accounts.
- 1Password: Helps you manage passwords, secure notes, and sensitive information with strong encryption.

1. Calendar and Scheduling:

- Google Calendar: A user-friendly calendar app to schedule tasks, events, and meetings.
- Calendly: Simplifies scheduling by allowing clients to book appointments based on your availability.

1. Project Management Suites:

- Monday.com: An all-in-one project management platform with customizable workflows and automation.
- ClickUp: Combines task management, docs, and time tracking in one versatile workspace.

1. Communication and Video Conferencing:

- Zoom: A popular video conferencing platform for virtual meetings and client consultations.
- Microsoft Teams: Offers video calls, chats, and collaboration within one integrated platform.

1. Email Management:

    - Gmail or Outlook: Use advanced features like labels, filters, and priority inbox to manage emails efficiently.
2. Automation Tools:
    - Zapier: Automates repetitive tasks by connecting different apps and services to trigger actions.
3. Mind Mapping:
    - MindMeister: Helps visually organize ideas and project plans through mind maps.

Choose the tools that best suit your workflow and needs. Integrating these tools into your freelance process can streamline your work, enhance collaboration, and increase productivity, allowing you to focus more on delivering excellent results to your clients in the gig economy.

- Avoiding Burnout and Maintaining Work-Life Balance

The gig economy can be demanding, and as a freelancer, it's crucial to prioritize self-care and establish boundaries to prevent burnout and maintain a healthy work-life balance. Here are strategies to avoid burnout and find harmony in your freelance career:

1. Set Realistic Boundaries: Define specific work hours and avoid working excessively long hours. Communicate these boundaries to clients and stick to them to avoid overcommitment.
2. Prioritize Self-Care: Make time for regular breaks, exercise, and activities that promote relaxation and well-being. Taking care of your physical and mental health is essential for sustained productivity.
3. Practice Mindfulness: Incorporate mindfulness practices like meditation or deep breathing to reduce stress and increase focus.

4. Schedule Downtime: Allocate time in your schedule for hobbies, socializing, or spending time with loved ones. Make leisure activities a priority to recharge your energy.
5. Know When to Say No: Be selective about the projects you take on and decline those that do not align with your goals or values. Saying no to certain opportunities allows you to focus on projects that truly matter.
6. Delegate or Outsource: If possible, delegate non-essential tasks or outsource certain aspects of your work to lighten your workload.
7. Take Regular Breaks: Step away from your workspace periodically during the day to refresh your mind. Short breaks can increase productivity and creativity.
8. Create a Dedicated Workspace: Establish a designated workspace at home or in a coworking space to separate work from personal life.
9. Plan Vacations or Staycations: Schedule time off for vacations or staycations to disconnect from work and enjoy a change of scenery.
10. Seek Support: Connect with other freelancers or join freelancer communities to share experiences, offer support, and gain insights on maintaining work-life balance.
11. Limit Digital Overload: Reduce screen time outside of work hours to reduce digital overwhelm and improve overall well-being.
12. Learn to Recognize Burnout Signs: Be aware of signs of burnout, such as chronic fatigue, decreased motivation, or increased irritability. Recognizing these signs early allows you to take appropriate measures.
13. Review and Adjust: Regularly review your work-life balance and make adjustments as needed. Flexibility is key to adapting to changes in your work and personal life.

Remember that maintaining work-life balance is an ongoing process that requires mindfulness and intentionality. By prioritizing self-care, setting boundaries, and making time for activities outside of work, you can prevent burnout and cultivate a fulfilling and sustainable freelance career in the gig economy.

Chapter 10: Handling Contracts and Legal Matters

- Importance of Written Contracts and Agreements

In the gig economy, written contracts and agreements play a vital role in establishing clear expectations, protecting your rights, and maintaining professional relationships with clients. Here's why having written contracts is crucial for freelancers:

1. Clarity of Scope: A written contract clearly outlines the scope of work, project deliverables, and timelines. It prevents misunderstandings and ensures both parties have a shared understanding of the project's objectives.
2. Protecting Your Rights: Contracts include terms and conditions that protect your intellectual property rights, usage rights, and confidentiality. They also define payment terms and penalties for non-compliance.
3. Legal Enforcement: Written contracts are legally binding documents that provide recourse in case of disputes or breach of agreements. They give you a legal basis for seeking compensation or resolving conflicts.
4. Professionalism: Utilizing contracts demonstrates professionalism and establishes your credibility as a serious and reliable freelancer.
5. Managing Expectations: Contracts allow you to set clear expectations regarding revisions, communication protocols, and project milestones. This reduces the risk of scope creep and client dissatisfaction.
6. Building Trust: Clients appreciate the transparency and professionalism that come with a written contract. It fosters trust and confidence in your ability to deliver on promises.

7. Preventing Payment Issues: A contract clearly states the payment terms, including the amount, schedule, and preferred method of payment. This helps prevent payment disputes and late payments.
8. Establishing Terms for Termination: Contracts should outline the conditions under which either party can terminate the agreement, protecting you from abrupt project cancellations.
9. Protecting Against Liability: Including liability clauses in contracts can help protect you from legal claims arising from accidents, errors, or omissions.
10. Adapting to Changes: Contracts provide a foundation for handling changes or additions to the project scope through change orders or amendments.
11. International Freelancing: When working with clients from different countries, contracts help you navigate cross-border legal and regulatory complexities.
12. Professional Growth: Regularly working with contracts helps you become familiar with legal terms, negotiation skills, and understanding the importance of clear communication.
13. Documentation for Taxes: Contracts serve as essential documentation for tax purposes, ensuring accurate reporting of income and expenses.

It's essential to have a well-drafted, written contract for every freelance project, regardless of its size or duration. Consulting with a legal professional to create standardized contract templates or review client-specific agreements can provide additional protection and confidence in your freelance endeavors.

- Understanding Legal Rights and Responsibilities as a Freelancer

As a freelancer in the gig economy, it's crucial to have a clear understanding of your legal rights and responsibilities to protect yourself and your business. Here are some key legal aspects every freelancer should be aware of:

1. Business Structure: Decide on the legal structure of your freelance business, such as operating as a sole proprietor, forming an LLC, or incorporating. Each structure has different implications for taxes, liability, and personal assets.
2. Contractual Obligations: Familiarize yourself with the elements of a legally binding contract. Contracts should include the scope of work, payment terms, intellectual property rights, confidentiality, termination clauses, and other essential details.
3. Intellectual Property: Understand the ownership of intellectual property rights in your work. Clarify whether you retain ownership, grant a license, or transfer all rights to the client.
4. Copyright and Licensing: Know the copyright laws in your country and how they apply to your creative works. Specify the usage rights granted to clients in your contracts.
5. Tax Obligations: Be aware of your tax responsibilities as a freelancer, including income tax, self-employment tax, and any local or state tax obligations.
6. Invoicing and Payment Terms: Establish clear invoicing procedures and payment terms in your contracts to ensure timely and fair compensation for your services.
7. Liability and Insurance: Consider obtaining professional liability insurance to protect yourself in case of errors, omissions, or legal disputes related to your work.
8. Data Protection and Privacy: Adhere to data protection regulations when handling client information. Implement

security measures to safeguard sensitive data.

9. Health and Safety: Take necessary precautions to ensure your workspace is safe and meets health and safety standards.
10. Handling Disputes: Know how to handle disagreements or disputes with clients. Establish a process for resolving issues, which may include mediation or arbitration.
11. Freelancer Rights: Understand your rights as an independent contractor, including the right to control your work, set your schedule, and negotiate terms with clients.
12. Unpaid Invoices: Develop strategies for handling clients who fail to pay for your services. This may involve late fees, collections procedures, or legal action if necessary.
13. Insurance and Contracts Review: Consult with legal professionals or business advisors to review your contracts and insurance coverage to ensure they adequately protect your interests.

Staying informed about legal matters as a freelancer empowers you to make sound decisions and protect your business. Regularly update your knowledge of laws and regulations related to freelancing, and seek legal advice when needed. By proactively addressing legal aspects, you can operate your freelance business with confidence and minimize potential risks.

- Dealing with Disputes and Protecting Your Intellectual Property

Dealing with disputes and safeguarding your intellectual property are essential aspects of protecting your freelance business. Here's how to handle these matters effectively:

1. Dispute Resolution Clause: Include a dispute resolution clause in your contracts that outlines the steps to resolve

disagreements. Consider mediation or arbitration as a cost-effective and less adversarial alternative to litigation.

2. Professional Communication: Maintain open and professional communication with clients to address concerns promptly. Often, disputes arise due to miscommunication that can be resolved through dialogue.
3. Document Everything: Keep thorough records of project details, communication with clients, and any changes to the scope of work. This documentation can be valuable in case of disputes.
4. Seek Legal Advice: If a dispute escalates and becomes challenging to resolve, consult with a lawyer experienced in freelance and contract law. They can provide guidance on your rights and options.
5. Fulfill Contractual Obligations: Ensure you fulfill your contractual obligations diligently and professionally. Meeting deadlines and delivering high-quality work reduces the likelihood of disputes.
6. Intellectual Property (IP) Protection: Clearly define ownership and usage rights of your intellectual property in contracts. Consider registering copyrights or trademarks for additional protection.
7. Use Watermarks and Copyright Notices: If sharing work online or in proposals, consider using watermarks or copyright notices to indicate ownership and prevent unauthorized use.
8. Non-Disclosure Agreements (NDAs): When sharing sensitive information with clients, have them sign a Non-Disclosure Agreement to protect confidential data.
9. Monitor Unauthorized Use: Regularly monitor the internet for unauthorized use of your work. Utilize image search tools and specialized services to identify potential infringements.

10. Cease and Desist: If you discover unauthorized use of your intellectual property, send a cease and desist letter to the infringing party, demanding them to stop using your work without permission.
11. File DMCA Takedown Notices: For online infringements, file Digital Millennium Copyright Act (DMCA) takedown notices with the respective platforms to have infringing content removed.
12. Register Copyrights: Consider registering your creative works with the relevant copyright office. Registration strengthens your legal rights and enables you to pursue statutory damages and attorney fees in case of infringement.
13. Monitor Contracts Regularly: Regularly review your contracts to ensure they remain up-to-date and compliant with legal requirements. Make necessary revisions as your business grows and circumstances change.

By understanding your legal rights, proactively addressing disputes, and safeguarding your intellectual property, you can protect your freelance business and maintain a professional reputation in the gig economy. Being prepared and informed empowers you to handle legal matters effectively and focus on the creative and rewarding aspects of your freelancing career.

Chapter 11: Building Long-Term Client Relationships

- Providing Exceptional Customer Service

Building long-term client relationships is essential for sustained success in the gig economy. Exceptional customer service is the cornerstone of fostering loyalty and repeat business. Here's how to provide outstanding customer service to your clients:

1. Communicate Effectively: Maintain clear, prompt, and professional communication with clients. Respond to emails, messages, and inquiries promptly and keep them updated on project progress.
2. Listen to Client Needs: Actively listen to your clients to understand their requirements, concerns, and expectations. Tailor your services to meet their specific needs.
3. Set Realistic Expectations: Be transparent about what you can deliver and set realistic expectations from the outset. Avoid overpromising and underdelivering.
4. Be Reliable and Consistent: Consistently deliver high-quality work within agreed-upon deadlines. Reliability builds trust and confidence in your abilities.
5. Provide Value-Added Services: Go the extra mile to offer additional value to your clients. Suggest improvements or solutions that enhance their projects.
6. Personalize Your Service: Take the time to get to know your clients and their businesses. Personalize your interactions to demonstrate genuine care and interest.
7. Ask for Feedback: Request feedback from clients on completed projects. Use their input to improve your services and show that you value their opinions.

8. Handle Complaints Gracefully: Address complaints professionally and promptly. Apologize for any shortcomings and work to find a satisfactory resolution.
9. Express Gratitude: Show appreciation for your clients' trust and business. A simple thank-you note or gesture can go a long way in building rapport.
10. Offer Loyalty Incentives: Reward repeat clients with loyalty incentives, such as discounts or priority access to your services.
11. Maintain Professionalism: Uphold a high level of professionalism in all interactions, even during challenging situations. Avoid getting emotionally involved in disputes.
12. Stay Updated and Adaptable: Keep abreast of industry trends and evolving client needs. Be willing to adapt your services to stay relevant and competitive.
13. Follow Up After Projects: After completing a project, follow up with clients to ensure they are satisfied with the outcome. This reinforces your commitment to their success.

Building long-term client relationships requires dedication and a commitment to providing exceptional customer service. By focusing on the needs of your clients, delivering value, and maintaining professionalism, you can cultivate a loyal client base that continues to seek your expertise in the gig economy. Happy clients are more likely to recommend you to others and provide valuable referrals, contributing to the growth of your freelance business.

- Upselling and Maximizing Repeat Business

Upselling and maximizing repeat business are effective strategies to increase your revenue and foster long-term relationships with clients. Here are ways to upsell your services and encourage repeat business:

1. Identify Additional Needs: Stay attuned to your clients' evolving needs. Offer additional services or upgrades that complement their existing projects or address new challenges they are facing.
2. Offer Service Packages: Create service packages that bundle related offerings at a discounted rate. Presenting comprehensive packages can entice clients to invest more in your services.
3. Cross-Sell Relevant Services: Propose related services that enhance the value of the client's primary project. For example, if you design a website, offer SEO services to improve its online visibility.
4. Showcase Success Stories: Share case studies or testimonials that demonstrate the positive impact of your work. Highlight successful outcomes to instill confidence in clients seeking your services.
5. Loyalty Programs: Implement a loyalty program that rewards clients for repeat business or referrals. Offer discounts, exclusive access, or special perks as incentives.
6. Stay in Touch: Maintain regular communication with past clients. Send newsletters, updates, or personalized messages to remind them of your services and keep your brand top-of-mind.
7. Special Offers and Promotions: Periodically offer limited-time promotions or discounts to encourage clients to return for additional projects.
8. Provide Frequent Updates: Share industry insights, new service offerings, or relevant content with clients through email or social media. Demonstrating expertise keeps you relevant and encourages repeat engagement.
9. Client Education: Offer workshops, webinars, or resources to help clients improve their businesses. Educating clients on

industry trends and best practices builds trust and positions you as a valuable partner.

10. Request Referrals: Ask satisfied clients for referrals to potential new clients. Word-of-mouth recommendations can lead to high-quality leads.
11. Stay Available: Be responsive and available to clients even after a project is completed. Timely communication can lead to new opportunities or referrals.
12. Upsell During Projects: As you work on a project, identify opportunities to add value or expand the scope of work. Present these options to the client during the project timeline.
13. Provide Exceptional Results: Deliver outstanding results consistently. Clients who are delighted with your work are more likely to return and engage in upselling opportunities.

Upselling and maximizing repeat business should be approached with a focus on providing genuine value and meeting clients' needs. By offering relevant solutions, maintaining strong relationships, and consistently delivering excellent work, you can enhance client satisfaction and build a loyal client base in the gig economy.

• Strategies for Generating Referrals and Word-of-Mouth Marketing

Referrals and word-of-mouth marketing are powerful tools for expanding your freelance business. Satisfied clients who recommend your services can bring in high-quality leads. Here are strategies to generate referrals and foster word-of-mouth marketing:

1. Ask for Referrals: Don't be afraid to ask satisfied clients for referrals. Politely request that they recommend your services to their network if they were happy with your work.

2. Offer Incentives: Consider offering incentives to clients who refer new business to you. This can be in the form of a discount on future services or a special bonus for each successful referral.
3. Provide Shareable Content: Create content that clients can easily share with their networks. This could be informative blog posts, infographics, or visually appealing portfolio pieces.
4. Showcase Testimonials: Display positive testimonials from satisfied clients on your website or marketing materials. Testimonials build trust and credibility with potential clients.
5. Engage on Social Media: Be active on social media platforms, engage with your audience, and share valuable content. Social media interactions can lead to organic referrals.
6. Collaborate with Other Freelancers: Partner with complementary freelancers to offer integrated services. Referring each other's services can expand your reach and attract new clients.
7. Offer Referral Programs: Establish a formal referral program that rewards clients who refer new business to you. Make the program easy to understand and participate in.
8. Network Offline and Online: Attend industry events, workshops, and conferences to network with potential clients and fellow freelancers. Engaging in online forums or groups can also help build connections.
9. Provide Exceptional Results: Deliver outstanding work consistently. Clients who are thrilled with your services are more likely to recommend you to others.
10. Offer Value to Potential Referrals: Share helpful resources or insights with potential referrals even before they become clients. Demonstrating expertise and generosity can make a positive impression.

11. Thank Referrers: Show appreciation to clients who refer new business to you. A simple thank-you note or a personalized gesture goes a long way in strengthening relationships.
12. Create a Referral Request Template: Provide clients with a template they can use to introduce you to their contacts. Make it easy for them to refer you by providing key information.
13. Follow Up with Referrals: When you receive referrals, follow up promptly and professionally. Make the referral process smooth for both the referring client and the potential client.

Generating referrals and fostering word-of-mouth marketing requires a proactive and customer-centric approach. By consistently delivering exceptional service and engaging with your clients and community, you can harness the power of referrals to grow your freelance business in the gig economy.

Chapter 12: Retirement Savings and Investment Planning

• Retirement Options for Freelancers (e.g., IRAs, SEP-IRAs)

As a freelancer, planning for retirement is crucial to ensure financial security in the future. There are several retirement options available to freelancers, each with its own benefits and considerations. Here are common retirement plans freelancers can consider:

1. Traditional Individual Retirement Arrangement (IRA):

- An IRA allows freelancers to contribute pre-tax income, reducing their current taxable income.
- Contributions and earnings grow tax-deferred until withdrawal during retirement.
- Contributions may be tax-deductible, depending on income and participation in employer-sponsored retirement plans.

1. Roth Individual Retirement Arrangement (Roth IRA):

- A Roth IRA allows freelancers to contribute after-tax income, so withdrawals during retirement are tax-free.
- This option is beneficial for freelancers who expect to be in a higher tax bracket during retirement.

1. Simplified Employee Pension Individual Retirement Arrangement (SEP-IRA):

- SEP-IRAs are suitable for freelancers with no employees or only a few part-time employees.

- Contributions are made by the freelancer's business and are tax-deductible.
- The SEP-IRA allows higher contribution limits compared to traditional or Roth IRAs.

1. Solo 401(k) (Individual 401(k)):

- The Solo 401(k) is designed for self-employed individuals with no employees, except a spouse.
- It offers higher contribution limits than other retirement plans and allows for both employer and employee contributions.

1. SIMPLE IRA (Savings Incentive Match Plan for Employees):

- Suitable for freelancers with a small number of employees.
- Contributions are made by the freelancer's business and may be matched by the employer.

1. Self-Employed 401(k) (Individual 401(k)):
    - Similar to a Solo 401(k), but with additional provisions for self-employed individuals with no employees.

Considerations for Freelancers:

- Evaluate your income and financial goals to determine the most suitable retirement plan.
- Regularly contribute to retirement accounts to take advantage of tax benefits and compound growth.
- Review and adjust your retirement plan as your income and business circumstances change.
- Understand the contribution limits, deadlines, and

withdrawal rules for each retirement option.
- Seek advice from a financial advisor or tax professional to optimize your retirement planning.

Investing for retirement is a critical aspect of financial planning for freelancers. Choosing the right retirement plan and making consistent contributions will help secure your financial future and ensure a comfortable retirement in the gig economy.

- Importance of Long-Term Financial Planning

Long-term financial planning is essential for freelancers to achieve their financial goals and maintain financial security throughout their lives. Here are several reasons why long-term financial planning is crucial:

1. Retirement Security: Long-term financial planning allows freelancers to build a robust retirement nest egg. It ensures they have sufficient funds to maintain their desired lifestyle during retirement and not rely solely on government benefits.
2. Goal Achievement: Financial planning helps freelancers set and achieve their financial goals, whether it's buying a house, funding education for their children, or starting a business.
3. Risk Mitigation: By planning for the long term, freelancers can protect themselves and their families from unexpected events, such as disability, illness, or sudden loss of income.
4. Debt Management: A well-thought-out financial plan helps freelancers manage and reduce debt effectively, enabling them to save and invest more for the future.
5. Tax Efficiency: Long-term financial planning includes tax planning strategies that help freelancers optimize their tax liability and take advantage of available deductions and credits.
6. Investment Growth: Planning for the long term allows

freelancers to make informed investment decisions, maximizing the potential for their investments to grow over time.

7. Inflation Protection: Long-term financial planning considers the impact of inflation, ensuring that the purchasing power of savings and investments remains intact over the years.
8. Wealth Transfer: Freelancers can use long-term financial planning to structure their estate and facilitate the smooth transfer of wealth to their beneficiaries.
9. Peace of Mind: Having a solid financial plan in place provides freelancers with peace of mind, knowing that they are prepared for both the expected and unexpected financial challenges.
10. Adaptability: Long-term financial planning allows freelancers to adapt to changes in their financial situation and adjust their strategies as needed.
11. Financial Independence: Through diligent financial planning, freelancers can work towards achieving financial independence, giving them the freedom to make choices based on their preferences, not just financial constraints.
12. Legacy Planning: Planning for the long term allows freelancers to create a meaningful legacy for their loved ones or support charitable causes that are important to them.

In the unpredictable world of freelance work, long-term financial planning provides a sense of stability and control over one's financial future. By assessing current financial status, setting clear goals, and implementing strategies to achieve those goals, freelancers can navigate the challenges of the gig economy with confidence and build a secure and prosperous financial future.

- Balancing Present Income with Future Savings

Balancing present income with future savings is a critical aspect of financial planning for freelancers. While it's essential to meet current financial needs, saving for the future is equally important to ensure long-term financial security. Here are strategies to strike the right balance:

1. Create a Budget: Start by creating a budget that outlines your current income, expenses, and savings goals. Allocate a portion of your income to savings while still covering essential living expenses.
2. Pay Yourself First: Treat your savings as a non-negotiable expense. Set up automatic transfers to your retirement accounts and other savings vehicles as soon as you receive income.
3. Emergency Fund: Prioritize building an emergency fund that covers three to six months' worth of living expenses. This fund provides a financial safety net in case of unexpected events.
4. Set Realistic Savings Goals: Determine how much you need to save for retirement and other financial objectives. Break down these goals into manageable, achievable targets.
5. Live Below Your Means: Avoid excessive spending and focus on living below your means. Look for ways to reduce discretionary expenses without compromising your well-being.
6. Track Your Progress: Regularly monitor your income, expenses, and savings progress. Use financial tracking tools or apps to stay on top of your financial goals.
7. Prioritize High-Interest Debt: If you have high-interest debt, prioritize paying it off before focusing heavily on saving for retirement. Reducing debt will free up more funds for future savings.

8. Incremental Increases: As your income grows, increase your savings contributions accordingly. Gradually boosting your savings rate won't feel as drastic as trying to save a large percentage all at once.
9. Diversify Your Investments: Invest wisely in a diversified portfolio to achieve growth and mitigate risk over the long term. Consult with a financial advisor to tailor your investment strategy to your goals and risk tolerance.
10. Delay Gratification: Be mindful of impulse spending and prioritize long-term financial goals over short-term gratification.
11. Take Advantage of Tax-Advantaged Accounts: Maximize contributions to tax-advantaged retirement accounts like IRAs and 401(k)s to benefit from tax deferrals and potential employer matches.
12. Reevaluate Regularly: Reassess your financial plan regularly to adapt to changing circumstances and ensure it aligns with your evolving goals.

Balancing present income with future savings requires discipline and conscious decision-making. By focusing on both short-term needs and long-term financial security, freelancers can achieve a harmonious balance that leads to financial prosperity and a comfortable retirement in the gig economy.

Chapter 13: Insurance and Risk Management

- Types of Insurance Coverage for Independent Workers

As an independent worker, managing risks through insurance coverage is essential to protect yourself, your business, and your financial well-being. Here are some types of insurance coverage that are important for independent workers:

1. Professional Liability Insurance (Errors and Omissions Insurance):

- Protects you from claims related to professional negligence, errors, or omissions in your work.
- Coverage includes legal defense costs and settlements if a client alleges that your services led to financial losses or damages.

1. General Liability Insurance:

- Covers claims for bodily injury, property damage, and personal injury that may occur at your workspace or during client meetings.
- Helps protect you from lawsuits related to accidents or injuries that occur as part of your business operations.

1. Business Owner's Policy (BOP):
    - Combines general liability insurance and property insurance into one package, providing comprehensive coverage for common risks faced by small businesses, including independent workers.

2. Cyber Liability Insurance:

- Protects against data breaches, cyber-attacks, and other cyber-related risks.
- Covers costs associated with data recovery, notifying affected parties, and defending against potential lawsuits.

1. Health Insurance:

- Provides coverage for medical expenses, including doctor visits, hospital stays, and prescription drugs.
- Freelancers can explore individual health insurance plans or participate in health insurance marketplaces if available.

1. Disability Insurance:

- Replaces a portion of your income if you become disabled and unable to work due to illness or injury.
- Short-term and long-term disability insurance options are available.

1. Life Insurance:

- Provides financial support to your beneficiaries in the event of your death.
- Term life insurance offers coverage for a specific period, while permanent life insurance covers you for your entire life.

1. Workers' Compensation Insurance (for Freelancers with Employees):

- Required in some jurisdictions if you have employees working for you.

- Covers medical expenses and lost wages for employees who get injured or become ill on the job.

1. Commercial Auto Insurance (if You Use a Vehicle for Business):
    - Covers damages to your vehicle and liability for accidents while using it for business purposes.
2. Product Liability Insurance (if You Sell Products):
    - Protects against claims related to product defects, injuries, or damages caused by products you sell.
3. Umbrella Insurance:

- Offers additional liability coverage beyond the limits of your other insurance policies.
- Provides extra protection in case of major lawsuits or claims.

Choosing the right insurance coverage depends on the nature of your freelance work, the level of risk involved, and your budget. Assess your needs carefully and consider consulting with an insurance agent or broker to tailor a comprehensive insurance plan that safeguards your business and personal assets.

- Mitigating Risks and Protecting Your Freelance Business

Mitigating risks and protecting your freelance business is vital to ensure its sustainability and growth. Here are strategies to safeguard your business from potential risks:

1. Professionalism and Quality: Deliver high-quality work and maintain professionalism in all client interactions. Providing exceptional service reduces the risk of disputes and negative feedback.
2. Written Contracts: Always use written contracts that clearly

define the scope of work, project timelines, payment terms, and intellectual property rights. Contracts protect both you and your clients in case of disagreements.

3. Diversify Client Base: Avoid relying heavily on a single client or a few clients. Diversifying your client base spreads risk and minimizes the impact if a client relationship ends.
4. Emergency Fund: Build and maintain an emergency fund to cover unexpected expenses or temporary income disruptions. This fund acts as a financial buffer during challenging times.
5. Incorporate or Form an LLC: Consider establishing a legal entity such as an LLC to separate personal and business liabilities. This shields your personal assets from business-related risks.
6. Cybersecurity: Implement robust cybersecurity measures to protect sensitive client data and prevent cyber-attacks. Use secure passwords, encryption, and reliable software.
7. Backup Data Regularly: Regularly back up your important files and documents to protect against data loss due to hardware failure or cyber incidents.
8. Stay Informed: Stay up-to-date on industry trends, regulatory changes, and best practices. Knowledge empowers you to make informed decisions and adapt to evolving circumstances.
9. Continuous Learning: Invest in your professional development to enhance your skills and stay competitive in the gig economy.
10. Network and Collaborate: Networking with other freelancers and professionals can provide support and potential collaboration opportunities. A strong network can offer resources and referrals.
11. Maintain Insurance Coverage: Choose appropriate insurance coverage tailored to your specific business risks. This includes

professional liability, general liability, and any other relevant policies.

12. Regular Assessments: Conduct regular risk assessments to identify potential vulnerabilities in your business. Address weaknesses and implement measures to reduce risks.
13. Plan for Business Interruptions: Create a contingency plan for unexpected events, such as illness, natural disasters, or economic downturns. Outline steps to continue operations during disruptions.
14. Client Screening: Screen potential clients to ensure they are reputable and financially stable. Avoid working with clients with a history of payment issues or disputes.
15. Legal and Tax Compliance: Comply with all legal and tax requirements for your freelance business. Staying compliant minimizes the risk of legal issues and financial penalties.

Protecting your freelance business involves a combination of proactive measures, risk management strategies, and maintaining a strong focus on professionalism. By taking steps to mitigate risks and safeguard your business, you can build a solid foundation for long-term success in the dynamic gig economy.

- Understanding Liability and Professional Indemnity Insurance

Liability and professional indemnity insurance are crucial types of coverage for independent workers to protect against potential legal claims and financial losses. Here's a closer look at these insurance types:

1. Liability Insurance:

- Liability insurance provides coverage for claims related to bodily injury, property damage, and personal injury that may occur during the course of your business operations.

- If a client or a third party files a lawsuit against you, liability insurance can cover legal defense costs, settlements, or judgments up to the policy's limits.
- Common types of liability insurance include general liability and product liability insurance.

1. Professional Indemnity Insurance (Errors and Omissions Insurance):

- Professional indemnity insurance protects you from claims of professional negligence, errors, or omissions in your work.
- If a client alleges that your services led to financial losses or damages, this insurance can cover legal expenses and compensation owed to the client.
- Professional indemnity insurance is particularly important for freelancers who provide consulting, advice, or services that could have significant financial implications for their clients.

Key Points to Consider:

- Coverage Limits: Both liability and professional indemnity insurance policies come with coverage limits, which determine the maximum amount the insurance company will pay in case of a claim. Ensure that your coverage limits are adequate for your business's needs.
- Tailored Policies: Independent workers should seek insurance policies specifically designed for their profession or industry. Generic policies might not address the unique risks associated with freelancing.
- Contractual Requirements: Some clients may require you to have certain insurance coverage, including professional

indemnity, before entering into a contract. Ensure you meet any contractual obligations regarding insurance.

- Deductibles: Insurance policies often come with deductibles, which are the amounts you must pay out of pocket before the insurance coverage kicks in. Consider your financial capacity to handle deductibles when choosing a policy.
- Renewals and Updates: Regularly review and update your insurance coverage as your business evolves. Notify your insurance provider of any changes in your business operations to ensure you remain adequately protected.

Liability and professional indemnity insurance provide essential financial protection for freelancers against potential legal claims and unexpected liabilities. By securing these types of coverage, independent workers can focus on their work with greater peace of mind, knowing they have a safety net in case of unforeseen events.

Chapter 14: Scaling Your Freelance Business

• Strategies for Expanding Your Client Base

Scaling your freelance business involves growing your client base to increase revenue and opportunities. Here are effective strategies to expand your client base:

1. Referrals and Word-of-Mouth: Encourage satisfied clients to refer your services to their contacts. Word-of-mouth recommendations can lead to high-quality leads.
2. Networking: Attend industry events, seminars, and conferences to network with potential clients and other professionals. Engaging in online networking groups can also widen your reach.
3. Online Presence: Create a professional website showcasing your work, skills, and testimonials. Use social media platforms to share your expertise and engage with potential clients.
4. Content Marketing: Produce valuable and informative content through blogs, articles, or videos. Demonstrating expertise and providing insights can attract clients organically.
5. Guest Posting: Write guest posts for relevant blogs or publications in your industry. This can help you reach a new audience and establish credibility.
6. Portfolio Showcasing: Display a diverse and compelling portfolio of your work on your website. Clients want to see examples of your past projects and successes.
7. Specialization: Consider specializing in a niche where you excel. Being an expert in a specific area can attract clients

seeking specialized skills.

8. Cold Outreach: Reach out to potential clients directly via email or LinkedIn. Craft personalized messages that highlight how your services can address their specific needs.
9. Attend Virtual Events: Participate in online webinars, virtual conferences, and workshops to connect with potential clients from different locations.
10. Collaborate with Agencies: Partner with creative agencies or marketing firms that may need freelance support for their projects.
11. Offer Free Workshops or Webinars: Host educational sessions related to your expertise. This can showcase your skills and build trust with potential clients.
12. Testimonials and Case Studies: Collect positive testimonials and create case studies showcasing successful projects. These add credibility and build confidence in your abilities.
13. Respond Promptly: Respond to inquiries and messages promptly to demonstrate professionalism and reliability.
14. Local Networking: Network with businesses and professionals in your local area. Local clients may prefer to work with freelancers they can meet in person.
15. Offer Incentives: Consider offering limited-time discounts or special rates for first-time clients to encourage them to try your services.

Expanding your client base requires consistent effort, persistence, and a commitment to delivering excellent work. By combining various strategies and continuously marketing your skills, you can attract new clients and grow your freelance business in the gig economy.

- Hiring Subcontractors or Building a Team

As your freelance business grows, you may find it necessary to expand your capacity and take on more projects. This can be achieved by hiring subcontractors or building a team of freelancers to work alongside you. Here are important considerations when hiring subcontractors or building a team:

1. Assess Your Workload: Determine if the volume of work justifies bringing in additional help. Analyze your current projects and potential future workload to gauge the need for assistance.
2. Define Roles and Responsibilities: Clearly outline the roles and responsibilities of subcontractors or team members. Define the scope of their work and ensure alignment with your business goals.
3. Look for Complementary Skills: Seek subcontractors or team members whose skills complement yours. Building a team with diverse expertise can offer clients a comprehensive range of services.
4. Evaluate Experience and Portfolio: Review the experience and portfolio of potential subcontractors or team members to ensure they meet your quality standards.
5. Communication and Collaboration: Effective communication is crucial when working with subcontractors or a team. Establish channels for regular communication and collaboration.
6. Contracts and Agreements: Use written contracts or agreements to define terms and protect both parties. Specify payment terms, confidentiality, project deadlines, and ownership of work.
7. Quality Control: Set standards for the quality of work produced by subcontractors or team members. Regularly review their output to maintain consistency and meet client

expectations.

8. Training and Onboarding: Provide proper training and onboarding for new team members. Familiarize them with your processes, brand guidelines, and client communication protocols.
9. Project Management: Implement project management tools and processes to efficiently manage tasks, deadlines, and progress. This ensures everyone is on the same page and projects run smoothly.
10. Pay Fairly: Offer fair compensation to subcontractors or team members based on their expertise and the value they bring to your business.
11. Manage Workloads: Monitor workloads to avoid overloading your subcontractors or team members. Ensuring a healthy work-life balance is essential for long-term collaboration.
12. Cultivate a Positive Work Environment: Foster a positive work culture that encourages collaboration, creativity, and mutual support. A harmonious work environment leads to increased productivity.
13. Feedback and Growth: Provide constructive feedback to subcontractors or team members to help them improve and grow professionally. Encourage open dialogue and continuous improvement.
14. Legal and Tax Considerations: Comply with legal and tax requirements when hiring subcontractors or building a team. Consult with legal and financial professionals if needed.

Expanding your freelance business by hiring subcontractors or building a team can be a rewarding way to take on more projects and increase your capacity. With careful planning, effective communication, and a commitment to maintaining high-quality work, you can build a successful collaborative environment that benefits both your clients and your freelancing career.

- Assessing the Feasibility of Scaling Your Business

Scaling your freelance business is an exciting prospect, but it requires careful assessment to ensure it's feasible and sustainable. Here are important steps to evaluate the feasibility of scaling your business:

1. Current Workload and Revenue: Analyze your current workload and revenue to determine if there is consistent demand for your services. Scaling may be viable if you consistently have more work than you can handle.
2. Market Demand: Research the market to identify potential growth opportunities. Assess if there is a sufficient demand for your services and if the market can sustain your expansion.
3. Financial Analysis: Conduct a detailed financial analysis of your business. Consider the costs associated with scaling, including hiring subcontractors, marketing, and any necessary equipment or software.
4. Profit Margins: Examine your profit margins to ensure that scaling won't compromise your profitability. Look for opportunities to improve efficiency and reduce costs.
5. Scalable Business Model: Evaluate if your current business model is scalable. Consider how your services can be expanded without sacrificing quality or diluting your brand.
6. Client Retention: Assess your client retention rate. High client retention indicates that your clients are satisfied with your services and are likely to continue working with you as you scale.
7. Competition: Analyze the competitive landscape to understand how you can differentiate yourself in a crowded

market. Consider what unique value you can offer to attract and retain clients.

8. Infrastructure and Systems: Assess if your current infrastructure and systems can support the increased workload and collaboration with subcontractors or team members.
9. Time Management: Consider how scaling will impact your time management and work-life balance. Ensure that you can handle the added responsibilities and maintain a high level of service.
10. Risk Analysis: Identify potential risks and challenges associated with scaling your business. Develop contingency plans to address these risks effectively.
11. Legal and Regulatory Considerations: Understand any legal and regulatory requirements related to scaling your business, including hiring, contracts, and tax implications.
12. Customer Feedback: Gather feedback from existing clients to understand their needs and expectations. This can help you tailor your scaling efforts to better serve your target audience.
13. Personal Goals: Align your business growth plans with your personal goals. Consider if scaling is the right decision for your lifestyle, ambitions, and long-term aspirations.
14. Resources and Support: Assess the resources and support available to you, including financial resources, mentors, or advisors who can provide guidance during the scaling process.

By thoroughly evaluating the feasibility of scaling your freelance business, you can make informed decisions that set you up for success. A well-planned and strategic approach to scaling can lead to increased revenue, expanded opportunities, and a thriving freelancing career in the gig economy.

Chapter 15: Adapting to the Changing Gig Economy Landscape

- Embracing Technological Advancements

The gig economy landscape is constantly evolving, driven in large part by technological advancements. As a freelancer, embracing these technologies is crucial to stay competitive and relevant in the rapidly changing market. Here are ways to embrace technological advancements in the gig economy:

1. Online Platforms and Marketplaces: Utilize online platforms and marketplaces that connect freelancers with clients. These platforms make it easier to find new projects and expand your reach.
2. Virtual Collaboration Tools: Embrace virtual collaboration tools that facilitate communication and project management with clients and team members, regardless of their physical location.
3. Cloud-Based Services: Utilize cloud-based services for file storage, document sharing, and project backups. Cloud technology allows seamless access to your work from any device.
4. Automation and Productivity Tools: Explore automation tools to streamline repetitive tasks, such as invoicing, scheduling, and social media posting. Productivity apps can help manage your time more effectively.
5. Artificial Intelligence and Machine Learning: Stay informed about AI and machine learning technologies relevant to your industry. These technologies can optimize processes and provide valuable insights.
6. Online Payment Solutions: Offer multiple online payment

options for clients to improve convenience and speed up payment processing.

7. Virtual Reality and Augmented Reality: If relevant to your field, consider how virtual reality and augmented reality can enhance your services or create new opportunities.
8. Data Analytics: Leverage data analytics to gain insights into client preferences, market trends, and your own business performance. Data-driven decision-making can give you a competitive edge.
9. Remote Work Infrastructure: Set up a reliable remote work infrastructure, including high-speed internet, video conferencing capabilities, and cybersecurity measures.
10. Continuous Learning: Stay updated on technological advancements by investing in continuous learning. Take online courses, attend webinars, and participate in workshops to acquire new skills.
11. Mobile-Friendly Approach: Optimize your online presence for mobile devices. Many clients and users access websites and content through mobile platforms.
12. Social Media Marketing: Utilize social media platforms to showcase your work, interact with your audience, and build a strong personal brand.
13. Cybersecurity Awareness: Be vigilant about cybersecurity threats and protect your data and clients' information from potential breaches.
14. Adaptability: Embrace a mindset of adaptability and willingness to learn new technologies as they emerge. Flexibility in adopting new tools and methodologies will keep you ahead of the curve.
15. Collaboration with Tech Experts: Collaborate with tech experts or freelancers with specialized technological skills. Partnering with them can enhance your services and lead to

innovative projects.

By embracing technological advancements, freelancers can leverage the power of digital tools to optimize their workflows, deliver exceptional services, and seize new opportunities in the ever-evolving gig economy landscape. Being tech-savvy is a key differentiator in today's market, and continuous innovation is essential for success as an independent worker.

- Staying Updated with Industry Trends and Best Practices

In the fast-paced gig economy, staying updated with industry trends and best practices is essential for freelancers to remain competitive and relevant. Here are effective strategies to stay informed and ahead of the curve:

1. Industry Publications and Blogs: Subscribe to industry-specific publications, blogs, and newsletters. These sources often provide insights into emerging trends, best practices, and expert opinions.
2. Online Courses and Webinars: Enroll in online courses and webinars related to your field of expertise. These platforms offer opportunities for continuous learning and skill development.
3. Professional Associations and Forums: Join relevant professional associations and online forums to connect with peers and engage in discussions about industry trends and challenges.
4. Networking Events: Attend conferences, workshops, and networking events to meet other professionals in your field. These events often feature industry experts as speakers, providing valuable insights.
5. Social Media Groups: Join industry-specific social media

groups to stay updated with the latest news and discussions related to your niche.

6. Thought Leaders and Influencers: Follow thought leaders and influencers in your industry on social media platforms. They often share valuable insights and updates.
7. Podcasts: Listen to industry-related podcasts to gain valuable knowledge from experts and successful professionals.
8. Web Searches and Google Alerts: Regularly conduct web searches on topics related to your industry to find the latest news and developments. Set up Google Alerts for specific keywords to receive relevant updates directly in your inbox.
9. Client Feedback: Stay attuned to client feedback and suggestions. Their insights can provide valuable information about emerging needs and trends in your market.
10. Analyze Competitors: Keep an eye on your competitors to see how they are adapting to industry changes and learn from their successes and failures.
11. Industry Reports and Surveys: Look for industry reports and surveys that provide data and insights on market trends and client preferences.
12. Continuous Experimentation: Embrace a culture of continuous experimentation. Test new strategies and approaches to identify what works best for your freelance business.
13. Webinars and Thought Leadership Events: Participate in webinars and thought leadership events organized by industry leaders and reputable organizations.
14. Mentorship and Coaching: Seek mentorship or coaching from experienced professionals in your field. Their guidance can help you navigate industry challenges and identify growth opportunities.
15. Adapt and Iterate: Be open to adapting your approach based

on new information and insights. Continuously iterate on your strategies to improve your performance.

Staying updated with industry trends and best practices is a proactive approach to excel in the gig economy. Embrace a learning mindset, invest time in professional development, and actively seek opportunities to gain knowledge from a variety of sources. By staying informed and current, you can position yourself as a knowledgeable expert and attract clients who value your expertise in the ever-changing landscape of the gig economy.

- Preparing for the Future of Work in the Gig Economy

The future of work in the gig economy is dynamic and full of opportunities. To prepare for the challenges and embrace the possibilities, consider the following strategies:

1. Continuous Learning and Upskilling: Commit to lifelong learning and upskilling to stay relevant in your field. Embrace new technologies and acquire in-demand skills to adapt to changing market demands.
2. Agility and Flexibility: Cultivate an agile mindset and the ability to adapt quickly to new situations. Flexibility allows you to pivot, explore new avenues, and take advantage of emerging trends.
3. Personal Branding: Build a strong personal brand that showcases your expertise, values, and unique offerings. A solid brand can differentiate you from others and attract the right clients.
4. Embrace Remote Work: Prepare for the continued growth of remote work. Invest in a reliable remote work setup and develop effective communication and collaboration skills for virtual environments.

5. Focus on Customer Experience: Customer experience will become a crucial competitive advantage. Prioritize excellent client service to build long-term relationships and foster loyalty.
6. Diversify Income Streams: Explore opportunities to diversify your income streams. Consider passive income options, online courses, or digital products that align with your expertise.
7. Adapt to Gig Platforms: As gig platforms evolve, be open to new platforms that align with your skills and target audience. Stay informed about the latest platform trends and policies.
8. Prepare for Automation: Understand how automation may impact your industry and job functions. Identify tasks that can be automated and focus on high-value activities that require human expertise.
9. Emphasize Soft Skills: Cultivate essential soft skills like communication, emotional intelligence, and problem-solving. These skills are increasingly valuable in a gig economy driven by human connections.
10. Network and Collaborate: Strengthen your network and actively seek collaboration opportunities. Partnering with other freelancers or businesses can lead to innovative projects and broader reach.
11. Financial Planning: Secure your financial future by diligently managing your finances. Create a financial plan that accounts for irregular income, savings, retirement, and potential emergencies.
12. Embrace Diversity and Inclusion: Embrace diversity and inclusion in your freelance business. Recognize and celebrate the value of diverse perspectives and experiences.
13. Stay Ethical and Compliant: Uphold high ethical standards in your work and comply with legal and regulatory

requirements. Trust and integrity are essential in building lasting client relationships.

14. Monitor Global Trends: Keep an eye on global trends and geopolitical developments that may impact your industry or client base.
15. Embrace the Entrepreneurial Mindset: Think like an entrepreneur and seize opportunities. Embrace calculated risks, learn from failures, and view challenges as stepping stones to growth.

The future of work in the gig economy is characterized by change and innovation. By preparing for this evolving landscape, you position yourself for success and longevity as an independent worker. Embrace technological advancements, stay informed, and remain adaptable to thrive in the exciting world of freelance work.

Conclusion: Your Journey as a Gig Economy Entrepreneur

As you reach the end of this book, take a moment to reflect on your journey as a gig economy entrepreneur. Throughout the chapters, you have explored the intricacies of freelance work and the gig economy, gained insights into financial planning, tax implications, and retirement savings. You have also learned strategies for expanding your client base, embracing technological advancements, and preparing for the future of work in this ever-evolving landscape.

Reflect on your progress and achievements:

1. **Skills and Expertise**: Consider how you have identified your strengths, talents, and areas of expertise. Acknowledge the growth and improvements you have made in your skill set.

2. **Financial Management**: Evaluate your financial planning and budgeting. Have you established emergency funds and set clear financial goals? Celebrate your milestones in managing irregular income.
3. **Client Relationships**: Reflect on the client relationships you have built and the exceptional customer service you provided. Think about how you have maximized repeat business and generated referrals through your quality work.
4. **Technological Advancements**: Embrace the advancements you have adopted in your work. How have you utilized automation, collaboration tools, and online platforms to enhance your efficiency and reach?
5. **Continuous Learning**: Appreciate your commitment to continuous learning and staying updated with industry trends and best practices. Identify the new skills you have acquired and how you have remained relevant in a competitive gig economy.
6. **Team Building and Scaling**: Recognize the achievements in building a team of subcontractors or freelancers to support your growing business. Consider how your leadership has contributed to their success.
7. **Adapting to Change**: Acknowledge your adaptability and agility in embracing change and uncertainty. Reflect on the challenges you faced and how you overcame them.
8. **Personal Branding**: Contemplate the impact of your personal brand on your business. How have you positioned yourself as an expert in your niche, attracting clients who value your unique offerings?
9. **Client Success**: Celebrate the successes of your clients and how your services have positively impacted their businesses or lives.
10. **Vision for the Future**: Envision your future in the gig

economy. Set new goals and aspirations for your freelance career, considering the evolving trends and opportunities in the industry.

Remember that being a gig economy entrepreneur is a continuous journey of growth and learning. Embrace the lessons from this book and use them as stepping stones to further success. Stay curious, open to change, and committed to excellence in all your endeavors.

As you embark on the next phase of your journey, know that the gig economy offers a world of possibilities. Seize the opportunities, build meaningful connections, and keep pushing the boundaries of your potential. Your passion, dedication, and entrepreneurial spirit will continue to propel you forward in this exciting and dynamic world of freelance work.

Throughout your journey as a gig economy entrepreneur, one lesson stands out as a cornerstone of success: the importance of continuous learning and adaptation. In the rapidly changing landscape of freelance work and the gig economy, the ability to adapt and evolve is not just an advantage; it's a necessity.

Continuous Learning: As the gig economy evolves, so do the skills and knowledge required to thrive. Embracing a mindset of continuous learning allows you to stay up-to-date with industry trends, emerging technologies, and best practices. It equips you with the tools to remain competitive and relevant in a dynamic marketplace. Whether it's through online courses, webinars, industry events, or networking with peers, investing in your professional development is a powerful way to unlock new opportunities and refine your expertise.

Adaptation: The gig economy is marked by its fluidity, and the ability to adapt to change is a valuable asset. Embrace agility and flexibility, as they enable you to pivot, adjust strategies, and explore new avenues. By being open to experimentation and willing to step out of your comfort zone, you can seize emerging opportunities and overcome challenges.

Technology and Market Shifts: Technological advancements continue to shape the gig economy. Embracing new technologies can streamline your workflow, enhance communication with clients, and improve your overall productivity. Staying informed about market shifts, client preferences, and emerging niches enables you to position yourself strategically and tailor your services to meet evolving demands.

Embracing Failure: Continuous learning and adaptation often involve taking risks and trying new approaches. Sometimes, these attempts may not yield the desired outcomes. Embrace failure as a natural part of the learning process. Each experience provides valuable insights that can inform future decisions and refine your strategies.

Customer-Centric Approach: As you adapt and evolve, never lose sight of your clients' needs. A customer-centric approach allows you to build strong relationships, deliver exceptional service, and exceed expectations. Listening to client feedback and being responsive to their evolving requirements ensures that you remain in tune with the pulse of the market.

Dear Future Success as an Independent Worker in the Gig Economy,

Congratulations on embarking on this exciting journey as a gig economy entrepreneur! Your decision to venture into the world of freelance work is a testament to your courage, ambition, and determination to carve your path to success. As you step into this dynamic and ever-evolving landscape, we want to offer you words of encouragement and wisdom to support your future endeavors.

Believe in Yourself: You possess unique talents and skills that set you apart from others. Believe in your abilities and the value you bring to your clients. Embrace your strengths and be confident in your expertise.

Embrace Challenges: Challenges are stepping stones to growth and achievement. Embrace them with an open mind and a positive attitude. Each obstacle you overcome will shape you into a stronger, more resilient entrepreneur.

Learn from Experience: Every project, every client, and every interaction is an opportunity to learn and grow. Embrace the lessons, both successes, and failures. Use them as building blocks for continuous improvement.

Nurture Your Network: Building strong relationships with clients and peers is essential in the gig economy. Nurture your network, be authentic, and seek collaboration opportunities. Your connections will be a valuable source of support and inspiration.

Stay Adaptable: The gig economy is marked by change, but you have the power to adapt and evolve. Stay agile, embrace new technologies, and be open to exploring new niches and opportunities.

Prioritize Work-Life Balance: While entrepreneurship demands dedication, remember to prioritize work-life balance. Taking care of yourself physically and mentally allows you to bring your best self to your work.

Celebrate Your Achievements: Celebrate even the smallest milestones along your journey. Acknowledge your achievements, no matter how significant or minor. These celebrations will fuel your motivation and boost your confidence.

Seek Continuous Learning: As the gig economy evolves, so must your skills and knowledge. Seek continuous learning and invest in your professional development. It's an investment in your future success.

Embrace Your Unique Journey: Comparison is a thief of joy. Embrace your unique journey and progress at your own pace. Your path may differ from others, but it's an authentic reflection of your passions and goals.

Be Resilient: Challenges and setbacks are inevitable, but your resilience will carry you through. Dust yourself off, learn from the experience, and keep pushing forward. Your determination will propel you to greater heights.

Remember, you have chosen a path that empowers you to define your destiny. The gig economy offers a world of opportunities and possibilities. Embrace each day with enthusiasm, and know that you have the power to shape your future.

Your journey as an independent worker in the gig economy is an adventure filled with growth, success, and fulfillment. Embrace it with an entrepreneurial spirit, and remember that you have the potential to achieve greatness. We believe in you and the incredible contributions you will make in this exciting world of freelance work.

Wishing you a future filled with abundant success and prosperity!

With warmest regards,

Alex Thompson

Don't miss out!

Visit the website below and you can sign up to receive emails whenever Alex Thompson publishes a new book. There's no charge and no obligation.

https://books2read.com/r/B-A-FEPY-BOMMC

BOOKS 2 READ

Connecting independent readers to independent writers.

Also by Alex Thompson

Alex on Finance

Financial Freedom Roadmap - Achieving Early Retirement through the FIRE Movement
The Art of Strategic Innovation
Beyond Cash - The Evolution of Digital Payment Systems and the Future of Money
Preserving Wealth in Inflationary Times - Strategies for Protecting Your Financial Future

Standalone

Side Hustle Success: Unlocking Your Entrepreneurial Potential
Side Hustle Success: The Ultimate Guide to Passive and Financial Freedom
Mastering the Markets: Advanced Trading Strategies for Success and Ethical Trading Practices
Financial Fortitude
Mastering the Art of Upselling
The Financial Bullet Blueprint
Investing Demystified: A Beginner's Guide to Building Wealth in the Stock Market
Real Estate Riches: Building Wealth through Property Investment
How To Succeed as a Freelancer

www.ingramcontent.com/pod-product-compliance
Lightning Source LLC
LaVergne TN
LVHW090422210926
848480LV00002B/657
* 9 7 9 8 2 2 3 4 2 7 6 8 1 *